ALSO BY RUTA SEPETYS

Between Shades of Gray

Out of the Easy

Salt to the Sea

The Fountains of Silence

I Must Betray You

VIKING

An imprint of Penguin Random House LLC, New York

First published in the United States of America by Viking,
an imprint of Penguin Random House LLC, 2023

Visit us online at PenguinRandomHouse.com.

Library of Congress Cataloging-in-Publication Data is available.

Printed in the USA

ISBN 9780593524381

1st Printing

LSCC

Design by Lucia Baez
Text set in Boston

This is a work of nonfiction. Some names and identifying details have been
changed.

The publisher does not have any control over and does not assume any
responsibility for author or third-party websites or their content.

For Michael

CONTENTS

INTRODUCTION

LIFE IS STORY IN MOTION.

Each day, you add to your story, revise it, and view it from a different angle. You erase things. Tear pages out. And sometimes, in hindsight, wish you could put them back.

A day is a story. A year is a story. A life is a story.

You are a story.

Whether you're writing fiction or nonfiction, the secret to strong writing is embedded within your own experience.

And your experience is rarely a one-person show. Hovering backstage are additional characters—family and friends—wedging in for a close-up. They create branches that lengthen and tangle your story. They add layers. If someone tells you that their family dynamics are perfect, I suggest you run. Because if their family is perfect, they're either incredibly boring or they're ashamed of Uncle Ron's sojourn in the nudist colony. And let's be honest, anyone who tears out the pages about Uncle Ron is boring.

The excitement of life dwells within the waves:

Heartbreak.   Hope.   Hilarity.   Humiliation.

The **H**'s are essential instruments in a writer's tool kit. We all have them. Your life journey has winding plots, unique settings, voice, and many characters. If you infuse those elements into your writing, it will feel authentic.

Because it is.

Prior to becoming a novelist, I spent more than twenty years in the music business. Working with songwriters, film composers, rock bands, and musicians was an education, to say the least. I had a bail bondsman on speed dial. But I also had something else—a front row seat to creativity.

And I noticed something. When the creators put a piece of themselves into their work, it was much more likely to become successful. The smallest kernel of emotional truth carried some sort of magical resonance. Suddenly, the song was relatable and affecting to the point that others claimed it as their own anthem. It struck a note both musical and personal. Listeners sang it in the car and thrust lighters in the air at concerts, saluting. It earned a spot on the soundtrack of their life. The elements were real and, as a result, had real impact.

Similarly, the road map for writing a book is embedded in your past experiences. Our failures, heartbreaks, and bad decisions are fabulous fodder for writing. The romantic interlude with the Amish guy, the escape from a D-lister's house in the Hollywood Hills, the job interview with the price tag hanging from the armpit of my suit—I would never tear those pages out of my story, and neither should you. They're color in a world too often steeped in gray.

Strong writing is rooted in emotion and imagination. The best writing inspires a vivid depth of feeling. Depth of feeling transports and transforms. It makes characters relatable and scenes unforgettable. Some writers believe they must create from nothing. But often, creating from nothing results in a feeling of the same. Nothing.

Over the course of this book, I'll share several components of story. I'll use examples from my own life and encourage you to contemplate yours. The concepts and presentation are intentionally basic, simple prompts to stir reflection and ideas. Since my experience is as a novelist, much of the content pertains to fiction writing. As the chapters progress, you may notice a layered effect, with themes from previous sections being incorporated through storytelling examples, essays, and assorted structure forms. And because I'm a writer who is passionate about history, I'll include some historical details for you to uncover and discover.

There are many methods of storytelling. To craft something memorable, I find it helpful to cross-examine my own memories and emotions and infuse those reflective elements into the building blocks of my story.

Of course, be gentle with yourself and use your own best judgment in deciding which memories to return to. But if you feel able, put a piece of yourself into the project. When you do, you'll pull the reader to the page and share something resonant and meaningful that will keep them there:

Heart.

PLOT

Plot Questions

WHY ARE SOME STORIES SO ENGAGING? Compelling plots invite the reader into an interesting setting, a burning secret, or a problem that must be solved. The crucial element of plotting is that the character has to *want* something. And the reader must know and understand that want.

As you think about your story, mull over these ten essential questions. Not all genres contain the following elements, but if you can answer these questions, you'll have a deeper understanding of your story.

INCITING INCIDENT
What event sets the plot into motion?

THE PRIZE
What does your main character want?

THE STRATEGY
What does your character decide
to do in order to get what they want?

THE CONFLICT
Who are some of the people
working against your character?

THE STAKES

What will be the consequence
if the plan does not work?

THE BLEAKEST MOMENT

What happens to make things look hopeless?

THE LESSON

What does your character learn
about themselves, others, or life?

THE DECISION

What does your character do
because of what they've learned?

THE HOLE

In what way does your character
need to grow emotionally?

THE BACKSTORY

What is haunting your character
as the story begins?

Over the course of life, we all move through a series of plots. Can you remember the inciting incidents, the strategies, the conflicts, and your bleakest moments? Take a minute to jot down a few bullet points. Or better yet, return to the place where you originally wrote them down. A diary, perhaps?

Personal Archives

WHEN DID THE DIARY DIE? WAS it suffocated with a pillow when I wasn't looking? A friend informed me that the journal has replaced the diary. Impossible! I have journals. They're mature. They're also whiny and boring. A diary is for confiding your most embarrassing secrets or your most profound fears. A diary is where you'll find the good stuff.

> **DI·A·RY** (noun): a confidential record of events in somebody's life, often including personal thoughts and observations
> **JOUR·NAL** (noun): somebody's written record of plans and postulates

I completely fabricated those definitions to support my point. To me, a diary and a journal just aren't the same. In a journal, you blather about the Camino de Santiago trek you'll take when the spirit moves you. In a diary, you confess you had a dream where you accidentally made out with your neighbor. In a journal, we write about what could be, or would be. In a diary, we write about what is. We stick to the facts. For example:

My brother drowned my Barbie. I snuck into his room and farted.

That's an entry from my old diary, about sibling revenge via gastrointestinal warfare. I find it uncomfortably revealing and I'm so glad I have it. Who was I back then? Can I apply or answer any of the ten plot questions?

The type of diaries I'm referring to had locks and miniature metal keys. I strategically glued a magnet beneath my bookshelf so my diary key would cling, completely out of sight. I was quite proud of that strategy. It never occurred to me that Mama Phyllis would pop the lock with a paper clip and read every last word. (Ciggy ashes between the pages gave her away.)

But diaries aren't just for children. While researching my books, I've read diaries of FBI agents, soldiers, and secret police that hold nothing back. Nothing. They're haunting and confessional. The conflict and stakes of the plot are instantly identifiable.

If your character kept a childhood diary, what would be in it? Would they have scribbled in the margins or crossed things out? Would they have written in code or would they feel safe to spill it all?

And what about you? If you could read anyone's diary, whose would you read and why?

What would you hope to find and how might it affect the plot?

When I find letters or diaries at estate sales, I snap them up immediately. I once discovered a bundle of old letters in a secondhand shop. The little sack of envelopes and postcards (all dating 1905–1910) was priced at only $1.50. They were gold.

> *Stanley, you must come at once. Meet me behind*
> *the post office at 7:00 p.m. on Tuesday.*
> *Tell no one! —Catherine*

It was signed and dated 1908.

Plot galore.

Why did Catherine summon Stanley to the post office? Why was it such a secret? What did Catherine want? Who was Stanley? Was he a cousin? School friend? Lover? *M u r d e r e r?*

I was hooked. Instant characters, plot, and stakes. And because I'm a research fanatic, I spent two years investigating until I finally uncovered the full story about Stanley and Catherine.

It was better than I ever could have imagined and inspired countless questions.

To build a strong plot, it helps to ask strong questions—questions that set a scene or encourage a detailed, creative response.

BORING QUESTION FOR STANLEY:
Describe something that once
happened at your job.

ENGAGING QUESTION FOR STANLEY:
Thinking back, did you ever take something home from
work or school that you weren't supposed to?

The engaging question sets a scene and begins to build a plot. Suddenly, we envision Stanley throwing a glance over his shoulder as he pinches a box of pens from the supply closet or stuffs paperwork down his pants.

Strong plots are often inspired by real-life events. And real life is full of engaging questions. The reality of life is so ludicrous, most will never believe it. It will feel fictional. Don't use names or exact details. You don't need to. Be creative. Don't write to condemn or call out. Instead, use the emotional stakes and quirks from actual situations to frame your questions and create your own composite plots.

As you think back on real-life scenarios, ask yourself: What did the person want? What were they willing to risk in order to get what they wanted? What was the hidden secret or the clue in the diary?

But what if no diary exists, you ask?

Perhaps it's not a book or digital device with daily thoughts, but you do have a diary. Old calendars, correspondence, and let's not forget old bill files. Financial records and receipts are dated. They often detail what you purchased, where, and even the time of day. Receipts contain the who, what, where, and when. Look at an old receipt, ask questions, and try to craft a new plot.

Why would someone buy a thousand Ping-Pong balls in Phoenix on March 12, 1999?

My accountant asked the same question. He felt a plot emerging. Or maybe an audit.

Of course, photos contain plot, but proceed with caution. Family photos often have a preexisting narrative attached to them. And sometimes that narrative can be photo fiction:

That's our son, Mark, at four. Our babysitter took
him to the mall to meet Santa. When it was his
turn, Mark was so excited that he cried!

Reach out to neighbors, friends, or relatives. Send them a few questions and note their recollections. Perhaps they have their own photos from the time period. Their photos and memories will present different angles of a story, plots that you've never heard:

> *Remember Mark's wicked babysitter, Becky? She*
> *hauled him to the mall under the guise of meeting*
> *Santa, but she really just wanted to see Sergio, who*
> *worked at Foot Locker. Mark was tired and com-*
> *plained. Becky pinched him so hard that he was*
> *still crying when he sat on Santa's lap.*

Same photo. Totally different plot.

And if photos, calendars, and receipts aren't enough, you have thousands of emails and texts that capture your opinions, your mind, your heart, and your daily doings of a time period. Revisit correspondence from years past. What were you discussing—and with whom? Did you ever have a secret or incognito email address? A PO box? If so, what was it for? What was the inciting incident? What was the prize? The bleakest moment? Visiting old material presents new perspectives and inspires fresh plots. Look at old photos or choose a photo on your phone. Invent an entirely new story around the image.

It's never too late to archive your own details. Document

your secret self for someone to discover in the future. Whether you use a snug book with a lock, a digital device with a password, or a message in a bottle, do it! Remain anonymous if you must, or create a pseudonym for fun. Plant clues. Imagine the mystery of finding a diary in the rafters of an attic, or better yet, the glove box of a car in a junkyard. Leave a trail for someone to discover and uncover.

Your story has value—and plot. As actress Mae West said in the film *Every Day's a Holiday*, "Keep a diary, and some day, it'll keep you."

Curiosity

INTERESTING PLOTS ARE POPULATED WITH INTERESTING people. Perhaps you were raised among unique folk or have met some along the way. Have they influenced your writing?

> LIST FIVE PEOPLE who have made a positive impact on your life.
> LIST FIVE PEOPLE who have made a negative impact on your life.

Positive and negative. Both are equally important because they drove your decisions and influenced the plot that is your life.

I'm the daughter of a Lithuanian father and a German American mother. Both struggled through hunger, hardship, and humiliation. More *H*'s.

My father was born in Lithuania and fled during World War II with his parents. He spent nine years in refugee camps before boarding a ship to New York. Upon arrival, his parents spoke no English and scrubbed toilets on Wall Street. After a year in Brooklyn, my grandfather was offered a job with Ford Motor Company. The family left New York and settled in Detroit.

My mother, the youngest of eleven children, grew up in the

inner city of Detroit. Her father was born in Germany, immigrated to the US, and worked as a laborer in Ford's auto foundry. He died at fifty-eight, before my mother's second birthday, plunging the family into poverty. My mother had a painfully difficult childhood and left school at fifteen in order to work and care for her ailing mother.

Despite their hardships, my parents became elegant, successful people—and successful parents. And I'm convinced it's because they were not only brave but also curious, and they passed that sense of wonder and adventure on to their kids. Mom loved books, music, and theater. Dad was a lifelong artist and soccer player who loved to travel. Because they had lost everything as children, they pursued life with a boundless sense of wonder and appreciation.

Their hardship had meaning and produced three spunky, venturesome kids. They had no impressive pedigrees, but somehow our parents matriculated and circulated amid an incredibly diverse group of people from the corporate world, to the creative world, to the underworld. And *that* was interesting.

I remember looking at an ornate sterling tea service that we never used. The card was still inside the sugar bowl. *For a Trim Little Philly from an Ole War Horse.*

"Where did this come from?" I asked.

"Jimmy Hoffa," replied my mother. "He gave it to me as a wedding gift."

Plot, anyone? But that was the end of the conversation. Temporarily.

My father owned a graphic design firm affiliated with an ad agency. The famed fashion writer for *The Detroit News* convinced my parents to buy a mid-century modern ranch in her neighborhood of writers, musicians, and artists. Every house in the neighborhood was its own encapsulated plot.

There was a Scandinavian auto designer who had a pet monkey, a doctor who gave martinis to trick-or-treaters, a family of architects who would become modern masters, an old ballerina whose entire house was carpeted in pink shag, and a babysitter who went to Hollywood and became famous. On weekends my father would travel with his soccer team for away games. He'd often return with some sort of injury. The martini-drinking doctor would sew him up while Mom stirred the Kraft mac and cheese and talked on the phone to the neighbor we were convinced was a spy. It all felt normal.

When I was in fifth grade, a girl I had met in mime class (see: boundless sense of wonder) came home with me. She looked around our living room and kitchen. Her brow wrinkled. "Ruta, you live . . . here?" she asked.

Her reaction confused me. Was she referring to the fact that my dad spoke Lithuanian, I had a strange name, and I was living in Michigan?

"I was born in Detroit. I'm actually American," I told her confidently.

"No, that's not what I mean."

What did she mean? And then I slowly understood. We were so insulated in our unique bubble. Our school was located within the subdivision. It was the first time I realized that maybe our home seemed odd to people who lived outside the neighborhood. Our kitchen wall featured a massive pop art illustration of a green hamburger. Our guest bathroom was painted glossy black and had a metallic print of Wonder Woman facing the toilet. We had tulip chairs and a bowl of white acrylic fruit. My father had created a silhouette portrait of his child—in neon.

My parents were conscientious and hardworking, but they were also interesting and expressive. Who signs their kid up for a mime class or builds an entire art installation for their son's beer can collection? The other families in the neighborhood did similar things. No one was rich, but they were rich with creativity and curiosity. And together, the families hatched endless stories and wild plots.

What were you curious about? Did your parents or relatives have any peculiar hobbies? Was there a mime in the family or a neighbor with a monkey? Which house was the oddball in the neighborhood? Whose house did you long to live in? Whose house was the party house? Whose house had plastic covering the living room furniture, or rules to follow? Think about the marriages, divorces, accidents, scandals, and triumphs. What do you remember about your community, and can you weave any of it into your plot?

When building your plot, remember two of the most important words:

WHAT IF . . .

    ❪ What if an unexpected package
showed up on your doorstep?
    ❪ What if it was leaking some sort
of liquid that was staining the porch?
    ❪ What if the name on the return address
was someone you thought . . . was dead?

Think of the community you grew up in and start brainstorming what-ifs. Let your curiosity fly.

Of course, there are mixed opinions on curiosity. E. M. Forster said, "Curiosity is one of the lowest of the human faculties. You will have noticed in daily life that when people are inquisitive they nearly always have bad memories and are usually stupid at bottom."

Maybe. But I prefer philosopher Piero Ferrucci's angle: "In the hidden folds of our life, we can find forgotten or unsuspected treasures which we have not appreciated for want of time or attention. They are the gifts of life, some apparently banal, some special. If we are distracted, we miss them; if we notice them, we are happier."

What resides in the hidden folds of your life? Shine light into those darker corners and see what you may find. Perhaps plot inspiration?

For your sake, I hope it's not a mime.

Conflict Layers

WHEN YOU'RE CRAFTING YOUR PLOT, IT helps to weave in conflict layers along the way. Conflict creates tension and intrigue. Conflict can appear in several forms in your story:

CHARACTER VS. ANOTHER PERSON

CHARACTER VS. SELF

CHARACTER VS. SOCIETY

CHARACTER VS. NATURE

CHARACTER VS. TECHNOLOGY

CHARACTER VS. MEMORY

I'll give you an example of conflict layers.

When I first began working in the music industry, I lived in Hollywood. I interned at a music management company and worked another job to make ends meet. Much of my time interning was spent in music clubs with the company's artists and writers.

One night, a band from New York that the company represented was in town playing at the Whisky a Go Go on Sunset Boulevard. I'll call them Band X. For the Whisky, this alternative band was unique at the time relative to the hair metal bands that frequented the club. They were irreverent, clever, and incredibly fun. And I loved them.

My job was to hang the band's posters around the club. I did, happily. I was twenty-two, had a brand-new business degree and my first job in the music business. The world was grand.

The headlining band was annoyed by my efforts to promote the opening band and had someone tear down the posters. When I told my boss what happened, I was nervous. Sweating. I stood in the corner of the band's dressing room while the guys complained that the headliners were pampered pricks. Their manager reminded them that their agent had pulled strings to get them this coveted opening spot at the Whisky, to play it cool, and not to repeat any of the previous episodes.

Previous episodes included being sued by Bozo the Clown, being jailed for obscenity, and the media reporting that Band X had chosen their name based on a phrase the singer scribbled down during his first shroom adventure.

CONFLICT LAYER 1
Prior episodes of conflict.

CONFLICT LAYER 2
A rivalry between bands.

CONFLICT LAYER 3

The agent had pulled favors to get them the gig.
Raises the stakes. The other manager agreed
and reminded the band that their previous arrest
had put the drummer's day job in jeopardy.

CONFLICT LAYER 4

The drummer's day job? He was a cop. With the NYPD.

CONFLICT LAYER 5

Location rivalry. LAPD vs. NYPD. There were mutterings and
complaints. Why not have a few cocktails to ease the tension?

CONFLICT LAYER 6

Alcohol. Why not? At some point, in the strange
citrus dream that is Los Angeles, someone told us
that the singer/satirist "Weird Al" Yankovic had arrived
for the show and was a big fan of the band.

CONFLICT LAYER 7

Random celebrity who attracts press attention.

By the time the band took to the stage, liquid courage prevailed. The show was great. The audience loved it. Energy was high. And then, during the final song, the singer slowly peeled off his shirt.

A bit pasty, but no problem. Lots of front men take off their shirts, right?

And then the trouser button was popped. Underwear peeked out at the crowd.

One of the managers grabbed my arm.

The crowd hooted and cheered.

"No," said the manager. "No, he won't."

Suddenly, Weird Al appeared onstage, put his leg behind his head, and began to pogo around while the front man dropped his pants and stood singing before us, in holy naked glory.

The audience stood, momentarily confused. Some cheered. Others shuddered. Someone chucked a beer at his crotch.

CONFLICT LAYER 8

Exposed genitals while people are throwing things.

The sound engineer grabbed a walkie-talkie. "Indecent exposure. Call the cops."

CONFLICT LAYER 9

Indecent exposure is a crime, punishable by law. Arrest.

RETURN TO CONFLICT LAYER 5

Location rivalry. LAPD vs. NYPD.

Note how every step of the way, a conflict layer was added. After the show, the managers grabbed the band to flee, but CONFLICT LAYER 6—alcohol—complicated transportation. We couldn't drive. We escaped to a hotel on the Sunset Strip and everyone hid in the bar. After a couple of rounds, I thought the ordeal had ended. I went to the restroom and a young woman who worked at the hotel eagerly asked if I was with Band X. "Is it them?"

I was so proud. Look at me, I'm a twenty-two-year-old Michigander in a fancy hotel on the Sunset Strip with a band that's all over MTV. "Yes, it's really them!" I whispered.

CONFLICT LAYER 10
Silly, starstruck intern who ruins everything.

Post-nudity episode, the band had fled to the hotel in hopes of remaining incognito. I eagerly confirmed their identity, and my eagerness resulted in, well, let's just say . . . problems.

As you build your plot, you want to add conflict layers. Conflict layers add obstacles and interruptions.

What kind of conflict layers have you faced in your own life? Do you have any allergies, phobias, or adversaries? Think back on those memories. Can you thread any of them into your plot and characters to create conflict?

Inclement weather would have been a great conflict layer in the Band X story. It rarely rains in Los Angeles, and when it does, it seriously complicates everything.

But that night, a naive intern brought the storm.

And she never forgot it.

PLOT · RECAP

❧

- Revisit your childhood self and the stories that reside there.

- Think back to your childhood home and community and how they shaped you. Whom or what did you love? Fear? Hate?

- Look for examples of plot in diaries and personal archives.

- Were there any families in your community who were their own encapsulated plot? Whose stories interested you?

- Ask yourself the essential question: What does the character want?

- Consider ways to ask engaging questions that set a scene or introduce conflict for your plot.

- Review old emails, correspondence, and receipts for ideas. A thousand Ping-Pong balls?

- Give thought to the curiosities and questions you still have.

- Brainstorm conflict layers and build them into the story.

- While building your plot, repeatedly ask, *What if . . .*

- Identify your main character's conflict. Is it with another person? Technology? Society?

- Look through the ten plot questions on page 6 and think about how they might relate to your project.

PLOT · WRITING PROMPTS

❧ You're attending a high school assembly. The power suddenly snaps off and the gym is plunged into darkness. When the lights flicker back on, the teachers suddenly realize _____

_____.

Fill in the blank and begin to create a plot.

❧ You borrow a book from the city library. When you arrive home and begin reading, you find a one-hundred-dollar bill between the pages. Along the edge of the bill is written, *Please help me*, along with a phone number. Answer the following questions with as much detail as you can:

Who is the main character?

What does the character want?

What are some potential obstacles and conflict layers?

What if . . . ?

❧ Write a fictional diary entry from the point of view of the person who finds the cash in the library book.

• Select a photograph from a book or a magazine. Write three radically different story captions for the photo that contain details relating to plot and conflict layers.

• Think of someone you'd like to meet or work with. Draft a list of creative, engaging questions for that person.

The Camino de Santiago

Each year, thousands of people from around the world challenge themselves physically, spiritually, and culturally to walk the Camino de Santiago. A network of ancient pilgrim routes, the Camino spans over five hundred miles. Many walkers report the journey as one that inspires friendships, memories, self-discovery, and story.

Q: Where are the routes located?

Jimmy Hoffa

The disappearance of Jimmy Hoffa is one of the most intriguing American mobster mysteries. A notorious labor union leader with reported Mafia ties, Hoffa suddenly disappeared without a trace. Over the years, people have come forward with various plots. Some claim they witnessed Hoffa's assassination, others confessed to burying him in a steel drum, and some swear he was entombed beneath Giants Stadium. But what's the real story behind the mystery of Jimmy Riddle Hoffa?

Q: What year did Hoffa disappear and what are the latest updates on the case?

Mid-Century Modern

Mid-century modern (MCM) is an American design movement that inspired unique architecture and product design. The original movement spanned 1945–1969, but the styles remain popular. Although some associate MCM with male designers and architects such as Eames, Saarinen, and Bertoia, it was a woman—Florence Knoll—who remains one of the most influential contributors. Orphaned at age twelve and educated in Michigan, Florence Knoll became a pioneer of the modernist movement and a crusader against gendered stereotypes in design.

Q: What defines the look of a mid-century modern house?

Hair Metal

Hair metal describes the catchy, good-time rock melodies performed by bands who sported teased hair in a fog of hair spray in the mid-1980s and early 1990s. This was a pejorative term initially created to discredit the artists, but many bands in the hair metal category have endured and still have successful touring careers. This subgenre of rock and metal birthed many uproarious tales and entertaining plots.

Q: Who are some artists in the hair metal category?

CHARACTER DEVELOPMENT

Rhythm

A HUMAN BEING I'VE NEVER MET stands in front of me at a book signing.

"I'm sorry, but I have to ask. This character—it feels like you based this character on me. Did you?"

I'm intrigued but confused. "I'm so pleased that you identified with the character, but this is the first time we've met, isn't it?" I ask.

"Yes. But I've always wanted to be in a book, and here I am in yours, well, in one of my past lives."

Between Shades of Gray, my book the young woman is referring to, is set in Siberia in 1941.

"Do you believe in psychic phenomena?" she whispers.

I've had enough experience with parapsychology to know that I don't have the gift. But I note the reader's mannerisms and her pattern of speech, and I can immediately tell which character she feels she represents.

Swiss psychiatrist Carl Jung presented concepts of what he termed *archetypes*—individual models that represent the structure of the human psyche. Jung believed that archetypes played a role in determining the personality. Twelve archetypes often associated with his work are:

THE INNOCENT	THE EXPLORER	THE MAGICIAN	THE JESTER
THE HERO	THE CREATOR	THE LOVER	THE CAREGIVER
THE OUTLAW	THE RULER	THE EVERYMAN	THE SAGE

Author Caroline Myss expanded upon the theory and presented more than seventy archetypes. Reviewing archetypes can certainly help create models for characters, but without specificity and rhythm, the characters will come across as flat, empty vessels.

Let's take rhythm.

Every human being has their own rhythm. When people imitate us, what they're imitating is our rhythmic patterns of speech, the rhythm of our movements, or the rhythm of a particular personality quirk we have. My mother had a unique rhythmic quirk— so unique that my friends remember it and can imitate it. Mom was legendary for her voicemail messages. The structure went like this:

> *Hi, love, it's me. [Insert some terrible, horrible news + thought.] Buh-bye!*

Hi, love, it's me. Do you remember your eighth grade algebra teacher? He set himself on fire in his garage yesterday. Awful way to go. Buh-bye!

Hi, love, it's me. A man in Ferndale drowned in his waterbed last night. Nasty things, waterbeds. Buh-bye!

Hi, love, it's me. The organist at church was found dead in his trunk. Turns out he was a crack dealer. Buh-bye!

The rhythmic archetype? The Bearer of Bad News.

Every human being has specific quirks. Maybe they're messy, a control freak, a gossip, a health nut, or maybe they're beautifully chill and naive. How do those quirks manifest in their rhythms, speech, and habits? Whether you're writing fiction, nonfiction, or a piece about your family history, show the reader the character's quirks and personality. Show them, don't tell them.

Example: an unpredictable person.

TELLING:
Kelsey's personality was a bit unpredictable.
SHOWING:
Being around Kelsey was like living with a grenade.
You never knew when she'd explode.

As you build your characters, think of the plot elements

we discussed. What does the character want? What are their obstacles? What are their secret dreams and fears? Are they shy or outgoing? Try to envision the characters as they speak, walk, and make decisions. Are they impulsive or methodical?

Remember, specificity is authenticity.

GENERAL:

He liked sports.

SPECIFIC:

Ted combed the internet
for sanctioned pickleball tournaments.

In the specific example, we learn more about the character. Can we envision the type of athlete drawn to pickleball? And the fact that he attends only sanctioned tournaments shows us even more.

Or—

GENERAL:

He liked sports.

SPECIFIC:

Jimbo hadn't missed a Steelers home game in twenty-five years.

You can tell the reader that your character likes sports. But when you get specific—Jimbo hadn't missed a Steelers game—it shows the reader so much more. It's no longer a general sports reference, but a specific sport, football. Suddenly, we have a location connection—Pennsylvania. We might also imagine something about his house. Does he have a Steelers sports den, or memorabilia crowding the walls? We even know a bit about Jimbo's schedule: he's watching football on Sunday. And we have an opening for deeper character development. Did he play football as a child or a teen? Attend or watch games with his family? Does he have black-and-gold clothing in his closet? Does he have recurring dreams of being in the end zone?

Specificity is authenticity. Look for places in your story where you can insert specifics about your characters. How can you show the reader more about them, their personal rhythms, speech patterns, the world they live in, and what motivates them?

If you include details that bring dimension and nuance to the characters you're presenting, they will feel real in such a way that the reader will recognize them or may even identify with them. The models all exist: the Workaholic, the Sloth, the Addict, the Angel, the Saboteur, the Servant—you recognize those archetypes. You've met them yourself. Maybe they were included on the list you created in the previous chapter of those who have impacted your life.

Think of their rhythms. You might not remember one sentence from this book, but tonight you might hear a song you haven't heard in five years, and you can sing every word to it. And that's because melody and rhythm are powerful. They're like sticky notes in your memory. Human rhythms function the same way.

Work with those memories; examine the characters in your past and present. Look at them from all angles and note the rhythms. Determine the role they play in the story that is your life. And as you do that, give thought to which archetype might best describe you. Discovering yourself is essential to discovering and building characters and stories.

Clarissa Pinkola Estés, who wrote *Women Who Run with the*

Wolves: Myths and Stories of the Wild Woman Archetype, urged us this way:

> I hope you will go out and let stories, that is life, happen to you, and that you will work with these stories . . . water them with your blood and tears and your laughter till they bloom, till you yourself burst into bloom.

Indeed. Work with your stories.

Water them with your blood and tears and laughter.

The world needs them.

The world needs more hearts in bloom.

BROWN CHAPTERS

❧

AT A PUBLISHING DINNER A FEW years back, an attendee asked:

"Ruta, you seem like such a happy person. Where does the darkness in your writing come from?"

Interesting question.

I've always loved moody novels. One of the first moody books I truly adored as a teenager was *Ethan Frome* by Edith Wharton, the story of a married man named Ethan who falls in love with his cousin Mattie. Mattie and Ethan realize that their forbidden devotion is a dead end. So, the two lovebirds sled down a hill to smash into a tree—a double death through which they will remain together forever. Yay! Except it all goes wrong and there is no happily ever after. Boo!

I loved it.

I read *Ethan Frome* when I was twelve, around the time I made the proclamation that no one understood me. I had felt that way since I was nine but formally announced it to my family when I was twelve. We refer to that time as "the brown chapter."

I confessed to my parents that upon turning thirteen, my new chapter in life might require a makeover of my bedroom.

Could I pay for it? they asked. (Children of immigrants don't get freebies.)

I had saved my nickels, had a humble budget, and was willing to use it.

Okay, then. Always eager to encourage expression and creativity, my parents agreed to explore the idea. My father, an artist, offered to sketch out a few designs for my new den of despondency.

"Brown!" I insisted. "Everything must be dark brown."

"Like chocolate," said my mother.

"No, like poop," I told her. "Brown like poop. Everything must be brown like poop."

Brown like poop. Can you imagine the thirteen-year-old character I'm describing? I insisted that even the insides of the drawers be painted brown. Metaphor galore.

"Brown." My father nodded gently. "Okay, let's explore that."

My father always treated young people with great respect, and he always believed in a plan. This was no different. He wanted more information. We sat in the kitchen beneath the green hamburger and he asked me a series of questions. I watched as he scratched notes on a yellow legal pad. He did the same thing with his design clients who wanted a corporate identity transformation. It all felt very official and exciting.

Did I agree to take part in the work? Oh, yes. Yes, of course, I assured them. My parents consented to brown as long as I'd compromise with an accent color. We settled on a soft shade of maize.

My bizarre boudoir had to blend with my parents' midcentury modern style. Not an easy task. But after several rounds of cigarettes and Sanka, Dad presented the ultimate design of despair. I was elated, thought it was a masterpiece, and found it well worth the pop of my entire piggy bank.

My new birthday bedroom included not only poop-brown walls but also a private sleeping chamber. My father installed a metal track on the ceiling surrounding my bed. We hung home-made curtains (brown, of course) from the ceiling all the way to the floor. This allowed me to completely close myself off when I needed a break from the world. The poop cocoon even had a reading lamp affixed to the wall so I could read and write until all hours of the night.

One of our neighbors stopped by and saw my new lair.

"It's very serious for a young girl, don't you think? And it's so . . . brown."

"I don't think you understand," I told her. "It's a brown chapter."

"Brown?" she asked, confused.

"Yes, very brown," I assured her.

The brown chapter lasted a couple of years and included dramatic diary entries describing my teen grief:

> *Don't ask me to write. Too painful.*
> and
> *Is love truth or is truth love?!*

In revisiting our showing vs. telling character development example—

TELLING:
She was a moody teenager.

SHOWING:

At thirteen, she painted her entire bedroom
a deep shade of fudge, even the insides of the drawers.
She christened it "the poop cocoon."

I marvel at my parents for allowing me to explore my inner mud. Now, as an adult, I don't like dark spaces. I prefer high ceilings and lots of bright, happy light.

But clearly, the moody girl must be lingering, because there's loads of family-inspired sadness in my novels. And there must be a couple smears of brown paint peeking through, because I still adore stories of desperation, tragic eternal love, and the not-so-happy ending. I love characters who struggle and fall short, who aren't exactly beautiful but have a beautiful capacity to love.

Sometimes, it hurts less if we decide that the precious and painful can be humorous. Perhaps that's what the guest at the publishing dinner was referring to. I love to laugh. Especially at myself. As Anne Lamott reminds us, laughter really is carbonated holiness. So I raise my guffaws to the gods, acknowledging that our ridiculousness can be riotous. Somewhere, one of my old neighbors is reminiscing about our neighborhood and they're probably saying, *Such characters. Remember the family with a monkey and that bizarre girl who lived in a creepy chocolate chamber?*

We all go through phases. The chapters of our childhood selves linger within our current selves. Give thought to that as you're creating your characters.

What chapter of life is your character in? What books would be on their shelf? What books do they love from childhood? Which characters do they identify with? What magazines do they subscribe to? Do they buy books at a local indie bookstore or from an online behemoth, or check them out of the library? What episodes from their past affect their present?

To answer the questions above, answer the questions yourself. What character from a novel did you identify with and why? Can you recognize elements of that character in yourself?

We all have brown chapters. And sometimes, they're simply too painful or traumatic to revisit. Use your own best judgment about which memories you might be able to responsibly dig through and which ones you should avoid. Protect your head and your heart. Always.

Sometimes, with a buffer of time, we look upon our brown chapters from a different altitude—one that inspires reflection more than reaction. When that happens, we might find meaning amid hardship and strength through struggle. And sometimes, what once seemed so dramatic and serious just might seem ridiculous.

Like a poop cocoon.

BACKSTORY

IN ADDITION TO CHARACTERS HAVING PERSONALITIES and rhythms, they also have backstories that drive their behavior and influence their decisions. Knowing a character's backstory gives context and helps the reader—and you, the writer—understand them. Backstory can also create great conflict layers for your plot . . . and your life.

To illustrate:

My parents rarely took vacations alone. They felt travel was transformative for young hearts and minds. When I was five years old, my mother rented a villa in Jamaica from Lord Ronald Graham. Lord Ronald was the brother of the Duke of Montrose and a proud Scot. He was also a bit of a character in the Caribbean. In addition to renting to my mother, he rented villas to the Manson Family and Marilyn Monroe. As the story goes, Lord Ronald had been recommended to Mom by "someone in the travel industry."

In hindsight, it sounds a bit sketchy. But remember my parents' backstories. As children, they both endured a lot. They were survivors, strong navigators, and circulated with diverse groups.

It was November when we departed chilly Detroit. We were a party of seven—my parents, my paternal grandparents, my two siblings, and me. In keeping with the Partridge Family trend of the time, our Lithuanian grandmother made matching travel outfits for us.

It was all so exciting. My very first flight. Going to sunny Jamaica in a snazzy turtleneck, tights, and a thick wool jumper. We would fly from Detroit to Miami and then from Miami on to Ocho Rios.

This was many moons ago, when flight attendants were called stewardesses, or stews. The Air Jamaica jet had a swanky gold cocktail bar in the center of the plane. Passengers were welcome to smoke fistfuls of cigarettes while airborne. Miniature rectangular ashtrays were built into the armrests to facilitate chain smoking. Seat belts? They felt optional. Air Jamaica heavily promoted its signature cocktail, the Rum Bamboozle. I wager my father and grandfather would have been the first to flash cash for it. But they didn't have to. Back then, it was all complimentary.

With Miami behind us, all the passengers were making merry. Steel drum music rolled through the cabin and the flight attendants began a tropical fashion show. The stews sashayed between the seats, presenting a myriad of vacation must-haves. All was well.

Until it wasn't.

The plane began descending, circling. Were we landing already?

Mom leaned out of her aisle seat. "What's he doing?"

One of the crew members was on his hands and knees, ripping up the orange carpet in the center aisle.

We knew the plane had beautiful flight attendants, a swanky bar, and lots of excited passengers.

What we didn't know was that upon takeoff from Miami, a tire blew on the landing gear. After some time in the air, it was discovered that pieces of the tire had flown into the plane's engine, damaging it. So while the steel drum fashion show was going on, the pilot was dumping fuel over the water and deciding where to make an emergency landing.

The fashion show ended abruptly. A crackly announcement was made.

"If you have children, please [feedback] your lap and cover them with [feedback]. Remove eyeglasses and dentures, bend at the waist, [feedback] between your legs. Brace for impact."

Brace for impact? Is that what the pilot said? It was so hard to hear.

It all happened so quickly. This was my first flight. Was this normal? My father and grandfather didn't catch the muffled announcement. Oblivious, they continued their rum-inspired conversation about communism, speaking loudly in Lithuanian. But some of the passengers looked frightened. The plane was listing. The next thing I remember was a smack landing, extended skidding with a peeling, screeching noise, and then—quiet. The passengers erupted into a frenzy of cheers and applause. Wow, flying was exciting!

The newspaper article reported that the pilots landed the DC-9 on a tilt, balancing first on one back tire, then lowering the belly down to a skid. The article also reported that the passengers on board were fairly calm although a bit frightened.

Upon deplaning in Kingston, Air Jamaica employees gave each passenger—including five-year-old me—a small bottle of rum.

"For your trouble, sweetie."

Fire trucks and ambulances lined the runway. Flashes of red lights. Commotion. I stood on the tarmac, clutching my bottle of rum. I was disoriented, and so hot in my turtleneck and woolen jumper. And all I could smell was jet fuel. What was happening?

Fast-forward and we're driving to Lord Ronald's villa in Ocho Rios. Mom sits next to me in the back seat. She smooths my hair and quietly asks if I'm okay. I nod. Sure, I'm okay. And then I promptly vomit all over my travel jumper, exorcist-style. They decide that I'm suffering from motion sickness.

As the years passed, I became airsick unless I was comatose on Dramamine. I traveled anyway but secretly wondered if it really was airsickness. The slightest whiff of jet fuel, even while on the ground, made me feel sick and like I couldn't breathe.

Backstory: childhood issues with planes and flying.

Backstories thread through our entire lives, and they should also thread through a character's life. They present surprises and obstacles that will enrich your story. My backstory with planes presented obstacles and, as I grew older, conflict layers.

In college, I studied in France for a year. I was beyond broke but loved it. As the year progressed, my dream was to spend my final summer living in Paris. But I needed money. I needed a job. For an American, it was extremely difficult to find a position and get a visa. I was qualified for practically nothing. A school advisor heard of a job opportunity that required a native English speaker. "Tell them I'll take it!" I exclaimed.

Characters who make rash decisions provide good conflict. The Paris job I was offered?

Working for Air France at Orly Airport.

"The Air France fleet is very distinguished," they told me. "They have the supersonic Concorde, you know. Of course, you won't be involved with the Concorde. You'll be working the five a.m. flights to Libya and Algeria."

Their words were noise to me.

What sort of cruel twist of fate was this? I desperately wanted to live in Paris for the summer. But I needed a job and money if I wanted to live in Paris for the summer. And that could all happen—if I spent most of my time around planes.

How would it work? People would notice my green complexion, wouldn't they? What were my options?

As you're crafting your story, try to push your characters into corners where they have to make a decision. If a character has a backstory that presents challenges, you'll have opportunities for decisions and conflict layers.

My choices at the time?

I could go home to Michigan and resume my sexy old employment. My main day job was working at Domino's Pizza. I also lit up phone lines selling furnace cleanings via telemarketing. Sure, I could return to those jobs.

Or I could live in Paris.

And spend the entire summer with my head in a toilet.

What was I going to do?

If your characters feel authentic, readers will become invested in their decision-making process. They'll understand the backstory and anticipate the unfair hurdles it might present. "Paris! Hooray! Wait. Oh no . . ." They'll suck in a breath as they turn the page. "She has to work for an airline? She can't work for an airline!"

I did work for an airline.

Air France provided the uniform: one red dress, one blue dress, one scarf, one navy sweater, and navy pumps. The photos of me in the crew flight lounge set the stage. The windows are wide open, planes are visible, parked at the gates close behind us. Engines roar above, rattling the chairs and tables. And we're all marinating—in jet fuel.

What elements of backstory weave in and out of your life? What were some of your very first jobs and whom did you meet there? Perhaps there are some people you'd like to meet again and others you secretly hope will be flattened by a bread truck. Can you infuse any of their personality quirks into your character development? Have you ever cried on the job or in public? Ever had a wacky internship? Have you ever quit on the spot and walked out? Has your backstory ever presented conflict at school or in the workplace?

Remember—backstory provides opportunity. Not only for challenge, but also for growth.

As Neil Gaiman wrote, capturing the sentiments of G. K. Chesterton: "Fairy tales are more than true: not because they tell us that dragons exist, but because they tell us that dragons can be beaten."

Backstory can also be beaten. And when it happens, it's glorious.

It was an epic summer.

CHARACTER DEVELOPMENT · RECAP

- Give thought to the people in your own life. Are you inspired to write about any of them?

- What elements of your childhood self still exist in your current self? What elements does your character still hold on to from childhood?

- Consider whether your character fits a certain archetype. Are they a Vampire, a Sage, a Savior? Or perhaps they're a unique hybrid and transcend all archetypal models?

- Look for places to gently infuse rhythm into your character descriptions.

- Incorporate showing, instead of telling, when describing your characters.

- Are there any elements of your life that you once found serious but now find hilarious? Are there ways that your character might take themselves too seriously?

- What phase of life or current "chapter" is your character experiencing?

- Remember, specificity is authenticity. Avoid general descriptions and drill to the details.

- Give thought to the backstory of your life and those you know. What obstacles, good fortune, or surprises has that backstory brought?

- What is your character's backstory and how might it affect the plot?

CHARACTER DEVELOPMENT WRITING PROMPTS

✎

- Think back to your childhood. Is there an experience that still affects you viscerally? A sound or smell that prompts a reaction or memory? Jot down details and consider how it might create backstory for a character.

- You discover that the school's maintenance supervisor is actually a magician from Poland. Make a list of character details and backstories. How might the discovery affect the plot?

- The following examples incorporate telling. Rewrite them to incorporate showing.

  Joe was really nervous.

  It was a cold day.

  I had the feeling he liked to dance.

- A character pulls into a high school parking lot but refuses to leave the car. List three possible backstories that would cause the character to remain in the car.

Consider these twelve archetypes: the Innocent, the Hero, the Outlaw, the Explorer, the Creator, the Ruler, the Magician, the Lover, the Everyman, the Jester, the Caregiver, and the Sage. Revisit your memories and the people you know. Create six more archetypes of your own.

Carl Jung

Are you an introvert or an extrovert? Do you ever try to interpret your dreams? If so, you're engaging in the work of Swiss psychiatrist Carl Jung. Jung was the founder of analytical psychology and developed the concepts of personality typology. His influential work includes theories on the conscious vs. the unconscious, archetypes, symbols, patterns, images, and dreams.

Q: Jung's work also refers to the shadow archetype. What does he mean by shadow?

The Manson Family

The crimes of the murderous Manson Family remain a scar on the collective memory of Los Angeles. Helmed by cult leader Charles Manson, the radicalized group included many interesting characters, including young women from suburban backgrounds. Manson Family stories include haunting episodes of assault, theft, and conspiracy, and they culminated with the grisly Tate-LaBianca murders in 1969.

Q: How many people were members of the Manson Family and how many were convicted of murder?

Edith Wharton

New Yorker Edith Wharton longed to become a writer during a time when women were discouraged from pursuits other than securing a husband. Wharton's mother disapproved of female novelists and her daughter's thirst for adventure. Wharton published her first novel at age forty, a year after her mother's death, and went on to publish classics such as *The Age of Innocence*, *The House of Mirth*, and *Ethan Frome*. She was the first woman to be awarded the Pulitzer Prize for Fiction and was also awarded a full membership in the American Academy of Arts and Letters.

Q: Besides writing, what was Edith Wharton's other notable talent?

The Partridge Family

A popular TV show in the 1970s, *The Partridge Family* featured a widowed mother managing the career of five singing siblings who toured in a funky patchwork bus. The fictional musical family was nominated for Best New Artist in the 1971 Grammy Awards, but in reality, only two of the actors took part in the music recordings.

Q: Which member of the Partridge Family became a teen idol and inspired mass hysteria at each appearance?

❧VOICE❧

Stylistic Identity

❦

OF ALL THE BUILDING BLOCKS AND elements of story, voice often feels the most elusive. So what is voice?

Voice is the tangible personality of your writing. It's the unique style and tone that will identify and differentiate you from others. If we think of music, are there singers or recording artists that you recognize from just a few notes? If we think of visual art, whose style is so uniquely defined that you could recognize it instantly? Perhaps Van Gogh? Keith Haring? Georgia O'Keeffe? If we think of architecture, maybe Frank Gehry, Gaudí, or Frank Lloyd Wright come to mind. That signature, stylistic identity—that's voice.

Imagine it this way:

You arrive home and on the kitchen counter are three typewritten letters, all unsigned. One is from your grandmother, one is from your best friend, and one is from a neighbor. Even though the letters are typewritten and unsigned, you can easily identify who wrote each note.

You recognize the voice. A sense of personality shines through the type.

Voice can appear in different ways: Writer's voice. Narrative voice. Genre voice.

⇒ WRITER'S VOICE ⇐

Some writers have a distinct style and signature delivery that carries through their entire body of work. With a signature writer's voice, you might identify the author from a single page. Examples of distinct writer's voice:

Jane Austen, Alice Walker, Theodor Geisel (Dr. Seuss), Roald Dahl

⇒ NARRATIVE VOICE ⇐

In some cases, authors create a narrator or main character with a strong voice who presents the story. Examples of strong narrative voice would be Claireece "Precious" Jones, the sixteen-year-old protagonist in *Push* by Sapphire, Death as the narrator in *The Book Thief* by Markus Zusak, or Holden Caulfield in J. D. Salinger's classic *The Catcher in the Rye.*

Personality and voice in writing can be created not only with text but also with rhythm. Recognize this voice?

Hi, love, it's me. Found a smashed rat under the couch cushion. Smelled like bad potato salad. Buh-bye!

Chances are you never met my mother, but at this point, perhaps you recognize the rhythm of her voice?

Another example of strong voice is Vladimir Nabokov. The opening of *Lolita* is haunting in tone, atmosphere, and rhythmic alliteration. Read this aloud, very slowly:

Lolita, light of my life, fire of my loins. My sin, my soul. Lo-lee-ta: the tip of the tongue taking a trip

of three steps down the palate to tap, at three,
on the teeth. Lo. Lee. Ta. She was Lo, plain Lo, in
the morning, standing four feet ten in one sock.
She was Lola in slacks. She was Dolly at school.
She was Dolores on the dotted line. But in my
arms she was always Lolita.

The voice of the narrator is so strong in *Lolita* that we can immediately picture him, almost hear him reciting the breathy prose beneath the narrow shadow of an unleafed tree.

⇒ GENRE VOICE ⇐

Certain writers become lighthouses of their genres. They work so well within a specific lane that they, themselves, define it for a time period:

STEPHEN KING: the voice of suspense, supernatural, and psychological terror
TONI MORRISON: the voice of American reality and Black culture
AGATHA CHRISTIE: the voice of mystery
MARY OLIVER: the voice of nature

Voice can also be established with punctuation, lack of punctuation, point of view, diction, syntax, or even by the way you use white space on the page. Let's imagine these examples are the opening lines of three different books:

VOICE EXAMPLE #1

. . . .

Hunted by her own guilt, Marcy Massengill presented
the possibility—followed by the probability—that her impending
death was, in fact, her own making.

In reading this voice above, can you imagine the narrator who might be speaking? The point of view is third person. There's a clip and tick to the voice and diction that's created by the extended sentence structure and the alliterative rhythm of *possibility, probability,* and *Marcy Massengill.* There's a personality of authority that comes through. Perhaps an archetype of a Detective or a Know-It-All.

VOICE EXAMPLE #2

. . . .

My mom had a thing about guilt, see,
she was frickin' hunted by it.

In reading the voice above, can you imagine this narrator? The point of view is first person. There's a relaxed annoyance to it. It's conversational. You can almost envision the narrator shaking their head or rolling their eyes as they speak. The archetype feels perhaps like that of a Slacker or a Frustrated Child.

VOICE EXAMPLE #3

. . . .

Guilt is a hunter.

Do not be fooled into thinking that to establish voice you need to be wordy. As Kurt Vonnegut proved, simplicity can bring tremendous emotional immediacy.

The third example is the opening line of my novel *Salt to the Sea*. I was striving for quiet darkness, an air of mystery about the narrator and the point of view. Perhaps the archetype of a Doomsday Confessor, setting the stage for downfall.

Over the years, some have described my work in the category of "genre voice"—a voice of hidden history. Regardless of genre, I do strive for a stylistic voice with my novels: an economy of phrasing. I try to pack a punch with simplicity and the fewest words possible. When I worked in the music industry, I noticed that some producers added layers of instruments to make a song sound big. But it didn't always work. Sometimes, it's the acoustic, solo voice that's the most moving.

So, you see, there is much elasticity in voice:

VOICE is color.

VOICE is space or lack of space.

VOICE is punctuation or rhythm or alliteration.

VOICE can make you feel comfortable or uncomfortable.

VOICE pulls you to the page and keeps you there.

VOICE is an element that's so strong, you can visualize the narrator and sometimes hear repeating refrains in your head.

Who in your life has a signature voice or style? Are there voices from your past that haunt you? Did anyone in your family have a "telephone voice" that was different than their true voice?

Do you know anyone who speaks differently in public than in private? What are some of the vocal elements that distinguished your teachers, mentors, or saboteurs? Imagine you're having a conversation with one of them. Write a few sentences and try to capture their voice as they express things to you, and then capture your own voice as you reply to them. What do you notice about the two different voices?

Whether writer's voice, narrative voice, or genre voice, voice is memorable.

And the foundation of voice is a sense of self.

Because *you* are memorable.

Yes. In fact, those who feel they are uninteresting are often the most interesting. But their humility might lead them to feel otherwise. They focus on others before themselves.

Sense of self comes from meetings in the mirror. Who are you and who do you long to become in this story we call life? Why did you pick up this book? Are you interested in writing? Why? Drill to the why. Listen to your inner voice. Listen to others speak about you and your experiences. Are their descriptions accurate or terribly inaccurate? How does that make you feel? Imagine inner voice in terms of archetype: the Vampire, the Innocent, the Hero, the Outlaw. What do those voices sound like?

Be patient while exploring the concept of voice. When I first began, I was writing a middle grade mystery novel. Following a critique at a writing conference, an editor requested the manuscript, so I decided to find an agent to represent the submission. I sent one exclusive query to an agent I greatly admired. He responded and invited me to send the manuscript. I was nervous. At the last minute, I decided to also send him five pages of a historical novel

I was playing with. I thought it might show a range of my ability. The agent phoned and explained that the middle grade mystery was good, might sell, but it was derivative. There were others like it in the market.

But the lonely five pages I had sent him?

He said the story was unique and that my passion for hidden history spoke loudly and urgently. He suggested I pursue that project instead.

I had completed a middle grade novel. An editor had requested it. I had spent years on the project. What to do?

I tossed the book aside and spent two years writing the historical novel instead.

And it changed my life.

It turns out that my authentic voice was in historical fiction.

When you're getting started, it's natural to explore voice through imitation. Because I love Roald Dahl, my original book was probably an attempt to emulate him. But with practice and exploration, you'll eventually find a style that feels so comfortable and resonant for you to write in, that you'll return to it again and again. It may take years. Decades. You may have to throw things out and start again. But it's worth it. Because along the way, you'll find your reason for writing; you'll find your purpose.

You'll find your voice.

Authentic Voice

FOR WRITERS, ESTABLISHING AND DIFFERENTIATING VOICE can be tricky. It sometimes involves ego or perception of your own life story. After all, an incident considered a failure by one person might be declared an exploration by another, right?

I've experienced both. What about you? Which do you cling to? Failure or exploration?

Have you always been an originator, or have you ever been an imitator?

When I was in fourth grade, it was discovered that I had a voice.

No, not a literary voice. My family called it "the devil voice."

For some odd reason, I was able to manipulate and throw my voice into different registers. I'd listen to a vocalization, note the timbre and rhythm, take a breath, and then spit out an imitation. My mother was absolutely enchanted. "You have a voice!"

I have clear memories of performing my vocal circus tricks during adult gatherings. Mom would yank me from a yellow-spined Nancy Drew book and stuff me behind a plant in the living room.

"When I give you the signal, do 'the voice.'"

The signal could have been the spark to light her smoke, or something more obvious, but when the signal came, I raised my voice and let it roar. And afterward, I was brought into the room for curtsies. Oh yes, indeed, that demonic, monster tone came out of this little thing with pigtails. Can you believe it? It wasn't always a dark or deep voice I imitated, but it was never a voice you'd expect from a little girl.

This was during the era of the suburban telephone—the original landline with no such thing as caller ID. If you were willing to shell out the money, you could dial any number. Anywhere. And someone on the other end would always pick up, having no idea who was calling.

During this time there was something known as a crank call, or a prank call. Of course, there was always the possibility of a wrong number, but a crank call was a dialing intentionally designed to dupe someone. And because caller ID didn't exist, it was entirely anonymous.

These days, conversations via cell phones are private. Back then, households had many extensions, so you could pick up a phone from multiple rooms and dial—or listen in.

My mother was delighted by crank calls. Not those we received from the heavy-breathing dialer we nicknamed the Huffer, but those she herself initiated, with her young daughter throwing her voice.

I would use the corded phone in the kitchen. My mother, perched with her ashtray, would listen in on the extension in her bedroom. I called car dealerships with "the voice," and sometimes created the narrative of an elderly man. I was Vern, had just turned eighty-one, had a fistful of lottery cash and wanted to spend it all on a truck. Today. Yes, we could make a cash deal. Today.

At Mom's prompting, I'd hustle the salesman into a fervor

and convince him to throw in a bottle of Harveys Bristol Cream if I pulled my money from the mattress and came down immediately.

Of course, Vern never arrived.

While Dad worked late nights at the design studio, Mom had me crank call her sisters, the neighbors, and even one of my teachers using "the voice." No one suspected it might be me.

Mom loved the sheer silliness of it. Her infectious laughter spurred me on.

When I was thirteen, it was determined that my voice could perhaps be used for singing instead of satanic incantation or swindling.

Mom scanned the ads in the county newspaper for a vocal coach. "Studies have shown that the human voice is fragile and should be handled with care," she announced.

I was game. Yes! Teach me! I wanted to sing songs I heard on the radio.

Enter Ms. Jan. The vocal coach.

My dear mother wanted to nurture my voice, but the only vocal coach she could find in our area was a prizewinner with the Detroit Metropolitan Opera.

Suddenly, my devil voice transformed into an operatic voice.

Let's return to the concepts of voice, failure vs. exploration, and imitation. Then step further back to our discussion of character development. Although I had thrown my voice for years, Jan the vocal teacher entered the scene when I was thirteen, during the brown chapter.

Here I was, a thirteen-year-old living in a poop cocoon, and along comes a shawled opera coach with an armload of librettos.

Opera is story. Very dramatic story.

And I was a very dramatic teenager. Imagine the worlds of emotion and melody colliding. My poor family.

Characters in operas were falling desperately in love, murdering each other, betraying each other, and rising from the dead. And they were doing it in jeweled slippers and puffy dresses. Marvelous!

Jan initially tolerated my vocal imitations but quickly pushed to identify my own range—the vocal register of my natural, most powerful voice.

We argued about it.

I preferred alto; it was easier to move in a lower register. The songs I liked to sing on the radio were in a lower range, mostly sung by men. Jan pointed out that my lower register was my imitation voice, not my own voice. But I had been imitating others for so long that I actually thought it was my *own* voice. Without realizing it, I had become an impersonator.

"You're much more than an entertaining party trick, my dear."

Jan's words stung my adolescent ego. But my mother agreed wholeheartedly. And Mom knew exactly which teenage buttons to push. Derivation was the easy way out. Originality was complex and deep. It required a unique element that most did not possess: grit.

Grit?

I was lacking grit?

My father, an immigrant, lost his country and spent nine years in refugee camps.

My mother, a survivor, lost her family compass and spent decades suffering.

Grit. Grit was passed down through DNA, wasn't it? And hey, did Mom no longer value the hilarity of our crank calls? Why were originality and voice suddenly so important? I pouted, convinced I was a failure. I cloistered myself in the poop cocoon, blasting my stereo with warbling opera LPs.

Jan had a residency, singing in the bar at an Italian restaurant. I begged my parents to take me. Chianti and cigarettes all around. But it was in that smoky bar at thirteen years old that I realized: originality *was* important.

Jan was entirely original. She was a coloratura soprano and sang like the most beautiful bird I'd ever heard. She referred to herself as Ms., a neutral, feminist title at the time. A single mother in the 1970s, Jan was fierce and immune to disapproval. She had emotional grit. Lush lyricism. And she delivered each aria as if standing on the bow of a sinking ship.

And this was not a stage persona. Jan carried a black lace fan, daily. She was the same person onstage that she was at the cheap piano in our house. Same rhinestone clips nested in her quivering pile of black hair. Same red lipstick, black stockings, and open-toed slingbacks. She was so passionate during our lessons that she'd sweat and her ample backside would literally stick to our piano bench. She was so passionate during her performances that *I'd* sweat and cry while listening. She was entirely original, a unique voice. And she wanted me to find my own voice, too.

Jan coached me through middle school, through high school, and on to a college music scholarship. She attended my performances, fan fluttering like a lace butterfly. I was never good enough to perform commercially in the US but once sang the

Canadian national anthem over the border in Windsor for a bankrupt liquor distributor.

All this to emphasize—voice is a journey.

Ann Patchett once said, "Why is it that we understand playing the cello will require work, but we attribute writing to the magic of inspiration?"

Such is the case with voice. It requires exploration, failure, success, hard work, grit, and, most of all, emotional experience. Early on, a writer's voice is sometimes derivative or emulative. And that is the highest compliment to those you imitate. But your true voice is layered deep within your life experience and your memories. It's the voice of your old diary, the voice of your desperation, and sometimes the voice you hope no one else will hear. With voice, age is an asset.

As you'll learn through this book on story and memory, I am a voice of glorious, celebrated fiasco. I am a music scholarship student morphed into a business major who went broke in Paris, bottomed out in Hollywood, made horrible decisions, and eventually found her way. And through it all, I've learned that things I once perceived as failure were actually sacred instruction on the path to authentic voice.

Please. Do not ignore the failure in your story.

FAILURE is a compass.
FAILURE is self-realization.
FAILURE is a prerequisite to success.
FAILURE will lead you—to your true voice.

VOICE · RECAP

- Voice is the tangible personality of your writing. It's the unique style and tone that will identify and differentiate you from others.

- Whose style is so distinctive that you could recognize it instantly? What are the factors that contribute to that uniqueness?

- Who in your life has (or had) a signature voice or style? What do you remember about it?

- Voice can be established with punctuation, lack of punctuation, point of view, diction, and syntax. Or even by the way you use white space on the page.

- When you're getting started, it's natural to explore voice through imitation. But as you continue, read your work aloud. Is the rhythm and flow your own or someone else's?

- With voice, age is an asset. Voice is layered deep within your life experience.

- Failure is a prerequisite to success. The best route to defining voice is to write often and again.

VOICE · WRITING PROMPTS

❧

- Write out the lyrics to "Happy Birthday" (or another well-known song) in an original, stylistic voice, using varied punctuation and white space on the page.

- A character drops a fishbowl. It shatters and the goldfish goes flying. Write three sentences about it from the following perspectives, using a different voice style for each:

  - A pet store employee.

  - A neighbor who is feeding the fish while the family is away.

  - A goldfish serial killer.

- Below are just two sentences from *The Color Purple* by Alice Walker. How do these lines establish voice, and what might you expect from the novel?

  My mama dead. She die screaming and cussing.

- Revisit my description of Jan, the vocal coach. Write a few lines of narrative voice, how you imagine Jan would sound if she was the narrator of a story.

❧ Below is the title and subhead of an essay by David Sedaris. How do these lines establish voice and what might you expect in the essay?

Old Lady Down the Hall

Her name was Rocky. She was my neighbor. I hated her guts. She was my best friend.

Atoni Gaudí

Catalan architect Antoni Gaudí is celebrated for his inventive, free-flowing style. An early interest in nature influenced his choice of materials, unique approach, and architectural voice. Some describe his work as mind-bending and Surrealist.

Q: Where are most of Gaudí's works located?

Roald Dahl

British novelist Roald Dahl created beloved and eccentric characters. From Charlie Bucket in *Charlie and the Chocolate Factory* to Miss Trunchbull in *Matilda*, Dahl's creative voice continues to delight readers worldwide, ringing up book sales of more than 250 million copies.

Q: True or false? Roald Dahl was buried with his snooker cues, a bottle of red wine, chocolates, pencils, and a power saw.

Toni Morrison

"Love is or it ain't. Thin love ain't love at all."

Toni Morrison's exquisite voice as a writer and human being touches upon themes that stir the soul and speak to the power of the human spirit. She was a novelist, a professor, an editor of fiction, and the winner of countless awards including the Presidential Medal of Freedom and the Nobel Prize.

Q: What sort of voice did Toni Morrison's family use when the landlord set fire to their house?

Coloratura Soprano

Agile trills, vocal leaps, and beautiful melodic runs are the ornamentation that define the coloratura vocal register. Coloratura can be sung by singers of all genders, but the most common coloratura is the soprano. A lyric coloratura showcases a light, bright upper range, while a dramatic coloratura sings with intensity and lingering sustain.

Q: Can a human voice really shatter glass?

PERSPECTIVE

Vision

JUST AS VOICE IS AN ELEMENT of writing, so is vision. I could even argue that vision is more important. How we choose to see often frames our life. It also frames the story. Whether intentional or not, the writer's spirit, worldview, and life experience appear on the page. And every writer has a different perspective.

Difference in perspective is natural and human. As William Blake so beautifully expressed, "The tree which moves some to tears of joy is in the eyes of others only a green thing that stands in the way."

How are you framing your memories and your personal stories? From what perspective? Is failure a fascinating forest of exploration or a suckhole of soul death? What kind of narrative are you creating and assigning to your past and the world you live in? That vision and perspective will drive the voice of your writing. The perspective and voice of a cynic, for example, reads much differently than the perspective and voice of a dreamer. Which best suits the story and feels most natural to you?

Expressive writers are often reflective, self-examiners. They comb their emotions and consider alternate angles for their work. And keep in mind, creating an alternate angle can produce a plot point or a unique character trait.

Get in the habit of considering alternate angles. When looking at photographs from your past, ask yourself: What lies outside the frame? What am I not seeing? How could I see this differently? Apply the *What if* question we touched upon in an earlier chapter.

What if you chose to view your life and experience differently?

✎ List three mistakes you've made—
and why they were mistakes.
✎ Now list a benefit that came as a
result of each mistake.

As you're listing the benefits, you're reframing the event and attaching a positive outcome. You're viewing the event from a different point of view. Suddenly, it's a different story.

Life is full of compelling stories and experiences. And remember, what you might consider mundane, others will find fascinating. Familiarity has a way of stealing the sheen from our everyday existence. But when captured and recounted by a descriptive writer, a childhood in Paris, Tennessee, is richer and more interesting than the tale of a suburban girl who goes to Paris, France.

Harry Crews didn't have a writing room or a computer. He had a makeshift desk created with an old door propped on cinder blocks. Yet his tales of rural Georgia in *A Childhood: The Biography of a Place* are visceral and transporting:

> *He had one of those good country voices: part*
> *drunk, part hound dog, part angel.*

I can imagine the character that Crews is describing. I can

hear him, smell him, and understand the layered aspects of his personality. I want more.

All from one sentence.

Country life, cosmopolitan life, quiet life—all can be equally fascinating based on the writer's perspective and the details chosen.

Adventures like those of Jack Kerouac intimidate some. They feel that because they haven't experienced far-flung destinations or drama, they have nothing to write about. But that's not true at all. It could be argued that the sensitivity and heart of Kerouac's writing charms readers just as much as his beatnik adventures.

Remember, it's not *what* you're writing about, it's *how* you're writing about it.

How do you choose to see? Are you interested in soul-seeking adventure or are you more drawn to details of the human condition? Kerouac sipped scotch from a pill bottle and died of alcoholism at forty-seven with a Kennedy half-dollar taped to his navel. Grand quest or tragic demise? How do you see it and how could you describe it in a way that captivates readers and allows them to see and feel it, too?

Sift through your memories and examine your perspective.

Is your perspective that of a have or a have-not? Was there something your friends had that you didn't? Vice versa? What do you remember desperately wanting as a child or a teenager? What is your perspective now on those wants? How would the story have unfolded if you had received what you wanted? In hindsight, how could you see the situation differently?

I wanted white high-heeled boots and a Big Wheel Racer. I

also wanted an allowance. Didn't get any of it. But if I revisit my memories, I can still feel that want—the aching potential of it.

An allowance—the textured crispness of dollar bills in one hand and a Scholastic book fair catalog in the other. I can imagine the gritty sound and sensation of gravel flying, spinning out on that Big Wheel. And ooh, the fabulous strain on my chicken-leg ankles as I totter to the bus stop in my pole dancer boots.

In hindsight, it's probably a good thing that I was denied the glory of my wants. I can see a few perspectives:

Me: *If I had those boots, I'd no longer be invisible. Boys would notice me. Boys with names like Lance. Yes, Lance is sixteen, but remember, I'm a very mature twelve. That's what it said on my report card. If only I had those boots . . .*

The bus driver: *And through the snow here comes this four-foot nothin', wobbling like a drunk in some sort of stripper boots. Didn't take but a few steps and she went down. Hard. Foot danglin', cracked off at the ankle. I heard the parents are some sort of Eastern European types.*

The EMT: *I'm sorry, miss, there's no way around it. We'll have to cut the boots off to save your ankle. Excuse me? What do you mean you'll roll the dice?*

The mother: *Hi, love, it's me. Remember the time you broke your ankle and the bloody bone poked straight through your boot? That sweet EMT was hit by a car today. Buh-bye!*

Perhaps at this point you're thinking, *Vision and perspective, yes, but where do I start? With plot, character, or setting?* It's entirely up to you. If ten writers are given the same writing prompt, they'll start in different places and produce ten entirely different stories. And that's because every human being has their own unique perspective. Some things to consider:

  ☜ Whose story are you telling?

☜ What is the story about?

☜ Describe the plot in one sentence.

☜ Describe the essence of the story in just one word.

☜ What gives the story its power?

Review your answers to the questions above. Do you notice a particular focus within your replies? How are you *seeing* your story? Do your replies lean toward character, plot, or setting? If you feel a pull toward one, you might use that as your starting point.

Also important to consider: How do you feel about the elements you're writing about? What is your personal perspective and viewpoint? Are you seeing the elements from the inside out, or from a distance—from the outside in? Is the perspective from your current self or childhood self?

And in terms of focus, are you a person who notices detail? Rhinestone hair clips and black stockings? The humid scent of Jimbo's football chili? The cracking knees of the brittle ballerina on a field of pink shag? What details dwell in your memory?

In revisiting your memories, give thought to how you might apply a different point of view or reverse the angle. How you choose to frame things makes all the difference in your story and, sometimes, in your life.

And what about that dark forest of exploration—mistakes? Was there ever a time you thought you understood the perspective but were wrong entirely?

That lapse in framing, perspective, or discernment? It's happened to me.

Some label it humiliation. Others illumination.

I'll share an example and let you decide.

Let's Run a 5K

I ONCE KNEW A GIRL WHO was born on October 10.

At the time, it was forbidden to share her name, so in my mind I referred to her by her birthday: Ten-Ten.

I was volunteering at the prison as an inmate mentor. She was serving time at the prison for armed burglary.

Ten-Ten was a twenty-two-year-old white girl from the South who grew up hard and lived even harder. Her mother overdosed and died when Ten-Ten was only two years old. By the time she was sixteen, Ten-Ten had two children. At seventeen she was selling guns and running dope in Tennessee. Her father sold heroin, and when money was tight, he sold Ten-Ten.

By the time I met Ten-Ten, she had run not only a drug ring but also a prostitution ring. She had been arrested countless times, shot twice, and stabbed in the chest.

"Why do you have to volunteer in a prison?" asked my friend. "Can't you just run a 5K or donate some money?" At the time, I could barely run my saggy ham fifty yards. I was tired of teaching adjunct at local universities. So I decided to put my teaching time into a prison program helping inmates study decision-making skills.

When I arrived at the prison I went through intake and

fingerprinting with the rest of the mentors. Most were promptly corralled into a visitation area. A few of us were told to wait and informed that we'd be escorted to the maximum-security facility.

Maximum security?

They sat me in a room, handed me Ten-Ten's file, and gave me a few minutes to review her information and organize my notes for our first session. I perused the papers.

Assault, burglary, drug distribution, armed robbery, prostitution, etc.

My pulse began to tick. What was I thinking? I was the queen of fiasco and wrong turns. How could I possibly help someone with decision-making skills?

The door buzzed. A prison guard escorted her to the table.

Medium height. Pale, thin. Orange jumpsuit. Long frayed hair. Eyes ringed with black circles and life mileage. She had the look of an angry doll. The guard said it was my choice whether I wanted supervision.

"I'm fine," I replied, trying to sound cool and relaxed. I felt like I had swallowed a sock.

Ten-Ten kicked the metal chair into position and sat down. She flicked me a nod.

"Hey, Snow."

Snow? Was she talking to me?

I took a breath. I think I gave an introduction. I launched into my monologue about the rules and the program, stuttering that the difference between good decisions and bad decisions could mean life or death, jail or freedom. I was about to begin the standard questionnaire when I noticed the moisture from my fingers seeping through the paper. I wiped my hands on my pants and snuck a look at Ten-Ten. She was grinning, leaning back in the chair. She pounced on the pause.

"You drive drunk, Snow?" She stared, unblinking.

"What? No," I croaked, trying to speak through the sock.

"You shoplift, then?" she countered. I shook my head.

She dropped forward in the chair, leaned in, and grabbed the reins. "Then what the hell is this community service about?"

It had been three minutes and I was already failing. I dropped the papers on the table.

"Let's see. I want to contribute but I can't run a 5K."

It took a few minutes to register and then Ten-Ten started laughing uncontrollably. "I'm your 5K, baby!" she yelled. "I'm your charity run." She pointed to her chest. "Let the donations begin!"

I told her I would be there every Sunday for the next three months—twelve weeks total—to meet with her. She found that hysterical, too.

"Three months, my ass. I'll piss you off and then you'll be outta here."

"So don't piss me off," I told her.

I drove home completely rattled. What if the car accidentally slid into a ditch? If my car was in the shop, I wouldn't be able to go back, right? That evening I received an email from the program coordinator, thanking the mentors for their time. She also reminded us that the inmates participating had independently volunteered for the program. If they completed it, it might improve their library privileges or work detail. But—no pressure.

Sure.

For the next three months I drove out to the prison each Sunday. I became accustomed to the concertina wire coiling the top of the fence, the beeping metal detector, and waiting for Ten-Ten in the gray tiled room that smelled like freezer burn. We used her crimes within our lesson plans.

"Instead of beating him with a baseball bat, what might have been another way to approach the situation?" I would ask. She liked to change the subject or flip the question to me.

"You ever hit someone with a bat, Snow?"

"No."

"You ever thought about it?"

After a few meetings she learned that if we got through the lesson quickly, I was fine to chat for the remaining time. So she'd skate into the room with a grin, fly through the exercises, then complain that she couldn't smoke during our talk time.

She asked about my family and I shared the general descriptions permitted. She was intrigued to learn that my immigrant father had been kicked out of his first high school in Detroit and that my mother had dropped out altogether.

"Yeah, I dropped out, too," said Ten-Ten.

Wait. Oh my, I could help!

"You can earn your GED while you're serving," I said, clasping my hopeful hands together. "The prison has a program."

"Oh yeah? Your mama ever get her GED?" she asked.

My momentary silence. It spoke.

Ten-Ten narrowed her eyes, staring at me. Her expression suddenly softened. "Yeah. See, your mama, she was real busy—busy bein' a good mama. That's what happened, Snow."

As the weeks progressed, Ten-Ten shared her poetry and told me all about the horror novels she was reading. We joked that we were each going to run a 5K. She said she would do it smoking and handcuffed and still beat me. Ten-Ten asked questions about my life and gave advice when I'd share vague details. Sometimes she'd even incorporate the decision-making curriculum.

"I'd tell you to show 'em a 12 gauge, Snow, but according to these handouts here, that would be a bad decision for you. So let's consider other options."

I was so pleased with our sessions. I was contributing. I felt I was making a difference.

That was my perspective.

"Why do you call me Snow?" I finally asked.

She laughed. "You even know what snow is? Snow is booger sugar. Cocaine. You look like one of those suburban ladies I sold coke to."

She wouldn't change the nickname, said it was too late . . . unless I wanted to tell her my real name. No, that was against the rules.

Ten-Ten liked what she called "quote shit." She asked me to bring quotes and read them to her at the end of our sessions. She'd lean back, bullying the metal chair, paying close attention as I read. She was very opinionated about the quotes and their authors.

Kahlil Gibran was dismissed as "too thick," Rilke "too wussy," and Virginia Woolf "too quiet." She loved Charles Bukowski and was thrilled when I brought quote shit from Bukowski's muse, John Fante. On the rare occasion that something moved her, she'd shove a piece of paper across the table and ask me to write it down.

"I like my quote shit deep but simple," she'd tell me.

Yes, she was partial to ferocious simplicity, but also gravitated toward quotes about relationships, family, and destiny.

One spring Sunday Ten-Ten was tired. She complained she couldn't sleep the night prior because someone told her it was raining.

"When it's raining, it's the best time to roll something serious. No one's watching, see. Remember that, Snow. No one's on guard when it's pouring down rain. The cops, they don't wanna get wet. The night I blew down that gas station, it was stormin' like crazy."

I nodded. "You were thinking about robbery last night?"

She looked up, hurt. "No, dumbass. I was worried you were out there in the rain and someone might hurt you."

It was then that I realized—my lens wasn't quite calibrated.

The inmates who made it through the entire twelve weeks were allowed to attend a graduation party with their mentors and eat vending machine snacks. I presented Ten-Ten with a wrinkled certificate and the bag of pork rinds she had requested. I was definitely more excited than she was.

"You did it!" I said.

She looked at me hard and long. "Oh yeah, Snow? Who learned more?"

We stood, silent. I had volunteered for the prison program thinking I was the one with something to offer. But at that moment it was painfully clear that I had it all wrong. It wasn't humiliating; it was illuminating.

I was the student. Ten-Ten was the mentor.

She had shared hard-won perspective, perspective on wounds created by both weapons and humans. She had introduced me to an entirely new point of view and taught me so much.

When the thirty-minute celebration came to an end, she

thrust a folded piece of paper at me. "Here, take this." She gave a bored sigh. "Yeah. Well, thanks. Remember, Snow, lock your door when it rains."

They escorted her out of the room. She didn't look back at me. When I was finally alone, I opened the small scrap of paper.

You are nobody, and I might have been
somebody, and the road to each of us is love.
—quote shit from John Fante

Fast-forward many years. The older I get, the more I interrogate my perspectives, both past and present. My prison badge and the memory of Ten-Ten hang in my office.

Last night it rained. I made sure the doors were locked.

I still haven't run a 5K.

Point of View

TO EXPERIENCE LIFE DEEPLY AND FULLY, you don't need to jet to another continent. You can volunteer in your community, meet others in a different circumstance, look through their eyes, and consider their heart.

Consider their perspective.

Point of view filters the story and positions the description of the events. How close or far do you want the reader to be to the main characters and the story? Each option has advantages and disadvantages. Which is best for your project?

FIRST PERSON

The story is told from the inside out. The narrator lets you into their head. You see the story through their eyes and their own personal descriptions.

PRONOUNS USED
I, we

EXAMPLE
I could make a difference. That's what I thought.
I was an idiot, just didn't know it yet.

SECOND PERSON

The story is told to "you." Although more common in nonfiction, advertising copy, or instructional material, second person can also be used in fiction.

PRONOUN USED
You

EXAMPLE
You pull up to the prison and tell yourself the same lie. You're going to make a difference. Yes, you will.

THIRD PERSON

The story is told from the outside in. In third person omniscient, the narrator is all-knowing. In third person limited, the narrator is relating the experience of a specific character.

PRONOUNS USED
He, she, they

EXAMPLE
Ruta was so sure. She thought she could make a difference.

If we were writing a story about Ten-Ten, the following are perspective options:

First person, from the mentor's point of view:
She called me Snow. She looked like an angry doll in an orange jumpsuit.

First person, from Ten-Ten's point of view:
I called her Snow. She was clueless, like the suburban ladies I sold coke to.

Second person, from the warden's point of view:
Three cement walls. You remember. You just don't want to admit it.

Third person limited, from the prison guard's point of view:
The inmate clearly had the upper hand—and she knew it. She was up to something.

Third person omniscient, from the security cameras' point of view:
The guard is distracted, hungry, and thinking about a cigarette. Ten-Ten slides her hand beneath the table and locates the taped item. Sharp. Snow has no idea what's coming for her.

Point of view is an important aspect of storytelling in any genre.

I write historical fiction, and history has many angles. To choose a perspective for my novels, I study the topic I'm writing about, pose questions about the nature of the events, and think deeply about whose point of view might best deliver the story, and in what tense. While researching my novel *Salt to the Sea*, it became clear that the history involved several countries. To represent the experiences of various cultures, I chose alternating first person perspectives of four different characters.

In the early stages of a project, I also evaluate perspective options that might deliver another angle on who is considered the main character. For example, in the story of Ten-Ten, some additional perspective options might be:

 ❧ Ten-Ten's cellmate.
❧ The gas station cashier
or a victim the night of her robbery.
❧ The high school guidance counselor who
encouraged Ten-Ten to stay in school.
❧ Ten-Ten's dead mother,
observing from the afterlife.
❧ Epistolary: letters from Ten-Ten's children.
❧ Members of the parole board,
in alternating perspectives.
❧ The program coordinator, observing my
interactions with Ten-Ten over twelve weeks.

Question your lens and how you're reflecting. Are you limiting yourself, stuck on one perspective? Memory can often be a holding tank for pain, shame, or sorrow. Your mind will try to use logic to push and sort through emotions. It will spin and spin, trying to make sense of things that don't make sense, insisting there's only one option. That's tiring. After a long wrestle, we sometimes lose hold of the rope and lose hold of the story.

Consider a different approach. If you feel able, face the memories head-on and dilute their power. Talk to them, write to them, and perhaps tell them they know nothing. Hold them at a different vantage point or choose an alternate narrator to tell the story. Find levity in the experience, if you can. As my parents' lives illustrate, we can't choose our hardships, but we can choose how we face our hardships. Create alternate angles and infuse the details into a new story.

Perspective is a choice.

Your choice.

PERSPECTIVE · RECAP

⚘ Whose story are you telling? Whose point of view?

⚘ What is the story about?

⚘ Describe the plot in one sentence.

⚘ Describe the essence of the story in just one word.

⚘ What gives your particular story its power?

⚘ Do you see the story from the inside out or the outside in?

⚘ Which aspect calls to you most urgently? Plot, character, or setting?

⚘ William Blake said, "As a man is, so he sees." How might that apply to your personal memories and to your characters?

⚘ Think of a time when you didn't see a situation clearly. What was your perspective then? What is your perspective now?

⚘ Familiarity steals the sheen from our everyday experiences. Remember, what is mundane to one person might be magical to another. You have a story and that story is worth telling.

PERSPECTIVE · WRITING PROMPTS

❧

❧ You sneak out of your bedroom window to meet someone you're not supposed to. Write a few sentences from the following perspectives:

> A. Third person limited: the parent or guardian who discovers you're not in your room.

> B. Third person omniscient: the new security cameras that record you escaping from the window.

> C. First person: the person who's waiting for you.

> Then revisit your sentences and add conflict layers.

❧ Choose a memory or an event from your life. Take a moment to consider a different perspective and look at it from the outside in. Write a description from the point of view of an outsider who is observing your life from the sidelines.

❧ In the story about Ten-Ten, consider the following:

> A. As a prison volunteer, what do I want?

B. What raises the stakes?

C. Identify a conflict layer.

D. Can you envision Ten-Ten as a multidimensional character? Why or why not?

E. What sort of feeling or perspective did the story leave you with?

✎ Choose a memory where you might have misjudged a situation. Write a paragraph about it in first person and third person. Which suits the memory and story best? Why?

The Beat Generation

Do you reject traditional perspectives and materialism? Are you a creative seeker with the heart of an explorer? If so, you might have gravitated toward the social and literary movement known as the Beat Generation. Originating in the 1950s, Allen Ginsberg, William S. Burroughs, and Jack Kerouac were a few of the central poets and writers who shaped the Beat Generation.

Q: Kerouac's most famous work, *On the Road*, is considered a roman à clef. What does that mean?

Prison Libraries

Prison libraries date back to 1790. Initially, books behind bars were limited to the Bible and prayer devotionals. But with time and the establishment of rehabilitation programs, providing newspapers, magazines, and books proved beneficial in promoting literacy and decision-making skills. Prison reading programs also benefit the inmates' families, facilitating connection and discussion through a shared experience with books.

Q: What type of degree must a librarian have to work in a correctional facility?

GED

The General Education Development test (GED) was developed in 1942. At the time, young people were being shipped off to war or sent into the workforce before they could finish high school. The test evaluates understanding of math, reading, science, and social studies. If passed, the GED provides certification that the test-taker has completed their high school–level education. Since its inception, more than twenty million students have graduated with the GED.

Q: Many successful and famous people have GEDs. Can you name a few?

Charles Bukowski

Nothing was off-limits for writer and poet Charles Bukowski. Nothing. In 1984, *Time* magazine hailed him as the "laureate of American lowlife." Although he passed away in 1994, each year Bukowski's irreverent writings find their way to a new audience. Vulgar to some, brilliant to others, his beloved, gritty musings on excess have sold millions and have also led to legendary quotes that are attributed to Bukowski but are often difficult to trace.

Q: "Great art is horseshit, buy tacos." Did Bukowski really say that?

❧SETTING❧

Immersive Atmosphere

SETTING IS MULTIFACETED.

It is location, time period, physical environment, historical era, and more. It's the place we run from, the place we return to. When done well, setting is an immersive, sensory experience that transports the reader to a place and time. It sets mood and tone, creates atmosphere, and becomes a character unto itself.

Consider the project you're envisioning—is it setting-specific, or is the setting simply a backdrop for a story that could take place anywhere? Think back to the settings and locations of your life. What emotions and sense memories do they evoke?

Where did you feel safe?
What do you remember about that place?
Where did you feel vulnerable?
What do you remember about that place?
What time period do you
associate with happiness?
What time period do you
associate with challenge?
Are there locations you
associate with particular people?

When evaluating options for setting, remember that geographic location, seasons, and local culture can influence characters and also create conflict layers. A character who ends up in Siberia during the winter, for example, must survive a conflict layer of cold and darkness. A character in New York might constantly fight conflict layers of traffic and crowded spaces. If your story is set during the summer, most schools aren't in session. If your story takes place over a holiday season, things are closed, schedules altered. All these setting-related elements will affect your story.

As you brainstorm about your project, take a moment to think back to your own settings. Write down the addresses where you've lived, people you lived with, the corresponding dates, and memories that come to mind. Review old photos and anchor your descriptions with detail. Just like characters, settings need detail to truly come alive.

What are the details you remember about a particular address? Maybe it's the dented mailbox, the smell that made you avoid the basement, or the discovery beneath the neighbor's porch. List as many specifics as you can remember. As you're doing that, pay attention to the feelings you associate with each location and setting. And because this book focuses on memory, we'll need to address an important topic: home.

Just because you lived at a specific location, setting, or residence doesn't necessarily make it a home. As much as home is a physical construction, it's also an emotional construction. As such, it's one of the most powerful settings in our memory and in our hearts.

What is the meaning of home to you—and to the characters

in your story? Where did you feel most at home?

> How would you, or your character, answer this
> question?
> Home is _____
> _____.
> Give as many different answers as you can.
>
> And then answer this:
> Home *was* _____
> _____.

We all define home differently. Throughout history and across the globe, home has represented different things to men than it has to women. Due to different gender expectations, men often associated the home setting as a place of rest, while women associated home as a place of work. With that in mind, how do you think your parents or guardians each would have defined home?

As we age, the home setting can have a clarifying or tangling effect. Some feel anchored at home, others unmoored. Peaceful or complicated. And as years progress, we come to view and recall home in new ways, closing a circle that echoes T. S. Eliot's theory that sometimes we arrive at the place we started and come to know that place for the first time.

How does your setting affect your characters, and how does your setting—past and present—affect you now? If you've ever returned to an old home or a former setting, did you find it the same or see it differently?

A changed perception of place—has that ever happened to you?

It happened to me.

I'll revisit the memories and fold them into a story example here.

The Setting Is Los Angeles

THE SETTING IS LOS ANGELES.

But it does not begin nor end there.

It begins in Michigan. I'm lying on a spongy, ancient mattress in my dorm room—a quiet dorm solely for women—and I'm deep in thought.

As I've mentioned, home for me was a suburb of Detroit, a creative neighborhood full of interesting characters. We were allowed to roam freely with the knowledge that we'd eventually wander back. If we didn't, our parents would bellow our name from the front door or call a neighbor to track us down. If we fell through the ice, someone would pull us from the pond. I felt comfortable and safe in Michigan. But my parents had made it very clear that once I graduated, I was on my own. My father gave me a book on writing business plans.

"You need a plan. Everyone does."

When I was nine, I had a plan. My dream was to become an author. I wrote my first novel in third grade but lost my courage when adults found my stories "inappropriate." So I decided to pursue music. Yes, my voice teacher had coached me into a small music scholarship, but once I arrived at college I faced the chilly truth.

I was barely mediocre. And sometimes, my singing was just plain bad.

At the time, my perception was that I had failed at writing and I had failed at singing. I needed a new North Star. This was my logic in pondering the predicament:

My vocal talent was thin, but I still loved music.
I also loved office supplies and ruled paper.
Music + office supplies = music business.

I promptly changed my major to international business. After returning from Paris, I completed my final semester and had to choose my next setting. My brother lived in Hollywood. There was a music scene there. So I packed up and moved to the left edge of the map.

Hollywood. Los Angeles County. California.

A lemon bath of bright light, home of the stars, a fabled city with a single season. But in the late '80s and early '90s, Hollywood wasn't glamorous. It was tired, gritty, and for a young woman low on funds, potentially dangerous.

Street hustlers were constantly prowling, blowing kisses and whispering offers to "smoke some rock" or "put a little taste in the pot." The iconic Hollywood haunts were overshadowed by Frederick's lingerie windows, the Scientology Celebrity Centre, and bus stops splattered with urine and hotline help numbers for runaways.

When I landed in LA, I didn't have a car, I didn't have money, and I didn't have a job. But I had a spiffy new business degree and, thanks to my flight crew experience, I knew how to wear a scarf. I took the bus to a Salvation Army store, scanned the racks for business casual, and bought the equivalent of a flight uniform: one navy skirt, one navy pair of pants, two shirts, one sweater, and a scarf.

This was pre-internet, so I also bought myself a copy of the *Los Angeles Times* and mailed résumés in response to several employment ads. While attending a music industry event with my brother, I met a musician from Wisconsin who happened to be house-sitting in the hills. I'll call him Clifford. Late forties, round spectacles, more scalp than hair, jelly waistline, leather sandals.

"Hey, there's a ton of space where I'm house-sitting. Why don't you crash for the week instead of sleeping on your brother's couch?" he suggested.

Everyone seemed to love Cliff. I had my pepper spray. Sure, why not?

At this point, I hope you're thinking back to the chapters on character decisions and plot.

The house was perched above Sunset Boulevard in the winding hills of Laurel Canyon. As we swirled and curled through the narrow streets, I marveled at the historic homes.

"Such good mojo in the canyon," said Cliff. "The Eagles, Joni Mitchell, the Doors, they all lived up here. Created beautiful music and art. Zappa had a great duck pond."

It was true, but did Cliff recall the *not-so-beautiful* events? The Manson Family murders took place nearby, and more recently, several people had been bludgeoned in the house of the Wonderland Gang. Yes, right in Laurel Canyon. The event was known as the Four on the Floor Murders and read like something from my mother's voicemail archive.

I stared out the open window trying to absorb the warm eucalyptus breeze and ignore the fact that Cliff had toed off his sandals and was now driving barefoot.

Los Angeles. Was I too uptight for LA? Too much of an introvert for LA? This wasn't a mistake, was it?

Our destination was understated—a faded wooden bungalow tucked into a snug of trees at the end of a buckled driveway. Cliff parked his windowless van on the street. A wave of laughter floated over a sloped hedge, followed by the shimmy of a tambourine. I trailed behind Cliff to the back. "Why aren't we going in the front door?" I asked.

"Oh, um, forgot my key," said Cliff.

Cliff had said there was "a ton of space." But space didn't mean bedrooms. There was one bedroom with a futon on the floor that Cliff offered to share with me. I politely declined. I later learned that Cliff's estimation of space was relative. He lived in his van.

"The couch in the office looks like a foldout. I'll take that," I told him. "Where's the homeowner?"

"Needed to get away. Chill for a bit. Say, how would you feel about a little photo shoot? I've got a great Pentax." He smiled and threw another cast. "I'm also great at foot massages."

My stomach clenched. "Oh, sorry, not my thing," I replied. "I've gotta finish my business plan."

"Focused. That's cool. There's some brownies and soup in the fridge; hammock on the patio's nice. I've invited a few friends over tonight. You're welcome to join. Just don't go in the garage."

I gave a half nod, making note to check out the garage as soon as possible.

The low-ceilinged bungalow, perhaps once hippie-cozy, smelled lonely. Inanimate. I took my bag to the small, dark office. Photos were missing from frames and the shag carpet had grown stiff for lack of tread. I opened a window. The assortment of LPs, books, and papers littering the office peeled back layers about the owner—Fleetwood Mac, Cat Stevens, photocopied notes on Ingo Swann's remote viewing, a Buddha figurine, and, next to an overflowing ashtray, a book called *How to Develop Your ESP Power.*

I settled in at the desk and began working. A jasmine-scented breeze began to mingle with the dust of dead memories in the room. And then I heard it. A rustling of bushes near the window, followed by the quick clicks—of Cliff's Pentax. What was he doing in the bushes?

Wait. Was he taking pictures of me? I quickly moved into the hallway.

Back pressed against the paneled wall and my heart beating, that's when the feeling first crept in, a feeling I would forever associate with the setting of Los Angeles.

Hypervigilance.

Early that evening, guests began arriving at the house. I met several musicians, a beautiful glassblower, and a Union Civil War soldier who had chosen to reincarnate as a CPA.

The group quickly surrendered to herb-inspired speculation about America's song "Tin Man." Breezy bright chords. *Smoke glass stain bright color . . . soapsuds green light bubbles . . .*

I quietly snuck into the garage.

A bare bulb threw weak light onto the scene. Positioned alone in the center of the concrete floor was a narrow bed with a clump of yellowed sheets. I threw a glance to the door behind me. Cliff's reminder whispered back to me. "Just don't go into the garage."

I stepped toward the bed.

An imprint of a head was still visible on the down pillow.

Next to the bed, a folding TV tray held an array of prescription bottles, a large plastic cup with a straw, a well-thumbed copy of Rumi, and a couple of pamphlets issued by the World Health Organization. The topic called out in block letters: AIDS.

Next to a metal shelf housing grass fertilizer and mousetraps was a suitcase and a pair of men's sneakers.

"He died."

Cliff's voice carried from the door.

"He died in that bed. The owner let him stay here."

I nodded.

But why was I nodding? I knew so little. The Midwestern news had reported AIDS as if it was something "over there." But it wasn't. It was right here. And there had to be more to the story. So much more. A terminally ill man had been living alone in a garage. He had died in a garage, accompanied by yard tools, a single light bulb, and what felt like an intimacy of loneliness. My bald ignorance and the sadness of the setting consumed me.

I left the garage, and soon after, left Cliff's bunkhouse. My first job was for an executive recruiting firm in Beverly Hills and then I worked as an intern and assistant for an artist management firm. And eventually, with the support of a mentor and the business plan that my father insisted I write, I opened my own music management firm. Despite the fact that I was gaining success and traction in my field, I was losing traction with the setting.

As beautiful as it was, Los Angeles required a heightened state of awareness, a constant hypervigilance that began to chip away at me. Solitude and quiet calm, I realized, were my greatest inspirations. Yet I had chosen a setting and a career that were in conflict with my soul. Any chance I had, I'd drive two hours to the desert, and spend time alone in wide-open, empty spaces. Amid the quiet of the desert, my thoughts returned often to the young man and the bed in the Laurel Canyon garage.

For many, Los Angeles is a glittering City of Angels. For me, it was challenging to forge deep friendships and manage the stress of curated lifestyles and hovering crime. My limited funds were an ever-present fence, and the traffic complicated everything. Attending a casual gathering could mean spending two hours in transit. Each way.

It was challenging, but looking back, I now see the setting was also a rich education full of history. I experienced the Rodney King riots, progress in treating AIDS and HIV, the devastating Northridge earthquake, misogyny in the music business, and O. J. Simpson's white Bronco chase. I was in a traffic jam when news radio announced that my former colleague from the recruiting firm had been murdered with Nicole Brown Simpson.

There was a pulsing, unforgettable surrealism to it all. It gripped me and depleted me, but I persevered. I tried to meet the challenges. A setting is what we make of it.

I finally bought a house, furnished the house, and planted pretty roses in the yard. Shortly thereafter, the house exploded with a shattering of glass and chaos in the dark of night. I stumbled from my bed into a beam of headlights blazing in the living room. A drunk driver had fallen asleep and plowed into my house. He fled the scene, leaving the car smoking and lights flickering. It took the police more than two hours to arrive.

I sat alone in my driveway that night and realized: I didn't have someone to pull me from the pond. My brother had left Los Angeles. I didn't date. I didn't know my neighbors. It would take my friends an hour to drive from the Valley to Santa Monica, and for some reason I didn't feel entirely comfortable asking them for help. If I became sick, would someone let me sleep in their garage? I wasn't sure.

In story construction, this is what's often referred to as the crisis event. Generally, the crisis event prompts soul-sized questions that inspire critical change.

It wasn't a hasty decision, but it was beautifully resolute. Sometimes the setting we choose just doesn't work. Or it works only for a period of time. And that's okay. We can start afresh. I rewrote my plan and chose a new setting. And once I did, everything slowly fell into place. I realized, as they say, it wasn't about trying harder; it was about resisting less.

I spent nearly fifteen years in a setting that delivered success but didn't nourish me. Do I regret it? Absolutely not. As Jane Austen said, "One does not love a place less for having suffered in it." A man I once interviewed for my novel *I Must Betray You* shared similar wisdom. He said his suffering was his greatest spiritual teacher.

Setting is also a spiritual teacher.

In Los Angeles, I learned about story, history, poverty, and the egoic self. I watched an old starlet put hemorrhoid cream on her face. I befriended a medium, learned the value of solitude, and experienced enough rock 'n' roll adventures to fill countless books. I love Los Angeles for giving me courage and a thick skin, for helping me find my center, and eventually find my way. I return to LA often and enjoy it immensely when I do. But I learned what didn't work for me. And that eventually drove me to another setting and other pursuits.

Years later at my hospice orientation, they asked why I wanted to volunteer and what I hoped to contribute. I didn't share the story of the Laurel Canyon garage, I just said that I hoped to keep people company as they transitioned from one setting to the next.

Somewhere, if Cliff's still roaming the planet in his van, he has photos of me. Photos he snapped through the bushes and curtains. We'll call them "unauthorized portraits."

But the strange thing is, I'm curious to see them. Photos of a young, naive woman in a new and strange setting. Arriving at a temporary intersection on the road of life that would eventually point toward home.

The setting was Los Angeles.

It did not begin nor end there.

A jasmine-scented breeze mingles with the dust
of dead memories.

Sense of Place

THINK BACK TO THE SETTINGS OF your life. What memories return to you? How would you describe them now to capture your experience then? How would you establish a sense of place?

> . . . *left edge of the map.*
>   *Hollywood. Los Angeles County. California.*
> *A lemon bath of bright light, home of the stars, a*
> *fabled city with a single season.*

How would you describe the characters who populated the setting and still populate your memory?

> *I'll call him Clifford. Late forties, round*
> *spectacles, more scalp than hair, jelly waistline,*
> *leather sandals.*

What sort of details could you include that might give the reader a sense of the era or time period?

> *The assortment of LPs, books, and papers*
> *littering the office peeled back layers about*

the owner—Fleetwood Mac, Cat Stevens,
photocopied notes on Ingo Swann's remote
viewing, a Buddha figurine, and next to an
overflowing ashtray, a book called How to
Develop Your ESP Power.

Was there a crisis event associated with the setting you're thinking of? If so, what sort of change did it inspire?

I sat alone in my driveway that night and
realized: I didn't have someone to pull me from
the pond . . . If I became sick, would someone let
me sleep in their garage? I wasn't sure.

As you're making notes about your setting, yes, you'll want to include details about geography, weather, and architecture, but also include the quiet details that capture the setting to illustrate the unique way it lives in your memory—and will live in your character's memory.

Next to a metal shelf housing grass fertilizer and
mousetraps was a suitcase and a pair of men's
sneakers.

Use sensory details to describe the setting not only by sight, but also by sound and smell. Think of what you saw, what you smelled, and what you heard.

Bus stops splattered with urine and hotline help
numbers for runaways.

A jasmine-scented breeze began to mingle with
the dust of dead memories in the room.

Establish the role of your setting. Is it a permanent fixture or a passing pause? Is it another universe entirely? Perhaps, as master storyteller Rod Serling described, it's "another dimension, a land of both shadow and substance, of things and ideas." Peer through the keyhole. Then open the door of setting with the key of imagination and memory.

SETTING · RECAP

※

- Determine if your project is setting-specific or if the setting is a general backdrop.

- Anchor your setting with details and sensory description.

- Make a list of the various settings and locations of your life. What emotions and sense memories do they evoke?

- Give thought to the conflict layers your setting might introduce.

- What is the meaning of home to you?

- What is the meaning of home to the characters in your story?

- What role does setting play in your characters' backstories and your own backstory?

- Over the years, has your perception of a particular setting evolved? How do your past settings affect your life now?

- Tour some settings of your past. What do you see differently?

SETTING · WRITING PROMPTS

❦

- Recall a time when you thought, *What in the world am I doing here?* Write for ten minutes about that time. Describe the setting and your feelings there.

- The setting is your very first classroom. Describe what you see, hear, smell, touch, taste, and intuitively feel in the space.

- Close your eyes and think of the word *vacation* for a few moments. Allow memories of a place and time to filter in. What type of setting does *vacation* bring forth for you? Write a few paragraphs about a vacation setting.

- Describe a neighborhood or school you once returned to after the passage of time. How was it different or the same? Were the memories and emotions still intact? What did you feel and how did revisiting affect you?

- Think back to a specific time and place in your life that presented challenges. Where were you? List the emotions you associate with that experience and setting. Are they universal or personal? Can you weave any of them into your character's experience?

The Wonderland Gang

Running drugs and robbing rival gangs. Those were the preferred pastimes of five members and two associates in Los Angeles known as the Wonderland Gang. On July 1, 1981, four of them were discovered slain in the two-story house on Wonderland Avenue. Neighbors in the canyon reported hearing screams from the house in the middle of the night but ignored them as the rental home was often the site of loud parties.

Q: Which member of the Wonderland Gang was convicted of smuggling drugs in the corpses of fallen American soldiers?

The 1992 Los Angeles Riots

In 1992, a jury acquitted four Los Angeles police officers in the horrific beating of Black motorist Rodney King. Anger and shock over the acquittal ignited five days of violent rioting in Los Angeles that led to over fifty deaths, two thousand injuries, and twelve thousand arrests. Over a thousand buildings were damaged, services were halted, a curfew was put in place, and many city residents were unable to go to work or school. Thirty-five hundred federal soldiers were eventually brought in to occupy the city and restore order.

Q: In order to be classified a riot in the US, how many people must be involved in the gathering and disturbance?

Northridge Earthquake

January 17, 1994.

At exactly 4:30 a.m., the City of Los Angeles was rocked from sleep by a violent blind thrust earthquake that registered 6.7 magnitude. Roofs collapsed, freeways fell, and buildings buckled. In less than twenty seconds, billions of dollars in damage was incurred and more than a hundred thousand people were rendered temporarily homeless. The destructive quake led NASA and others to develop additional GPS stations to better map fault motions and predict the probability of future temblors.

Q: What is the largest earthquake in world history?

ESP

In the 1930s, a husband-and-wife team conducted a series of parapsychology experiments at Duke University to gather evidence of extrasensory perception (ESP). The experiments involved pairs of people. One person, the sender, looked at a symbol on a card, and the other, the receiver, tried to guess the symbol. Although skeptics abound, some have devoted their careers to studying mind reading and ESP. Even organizations such as the CIA have spent millions on ESP-related research.

Q: Is ESP the same thing as a sixth sense?

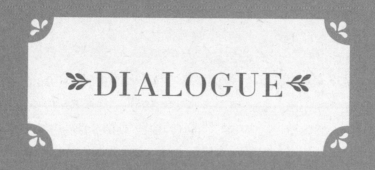

DIALOGUE

The Conversational Ear

DIALOGUE IS AN ESSENTIAL TOOL OF storytelling. And if it's well executed, dialogue is a sneaky facilitator. It's another element that works in concert. Dialogue can advance the plot, deepen character development, enhance emotion, or anchor a setting. We discussed that voice requires vision. Dialogue also requires something—the art of ear training.

People talk.

On most occasions we simply hear; we don't *listen*.

But even if we're not intentionally listening, these qualities often penetrate our ears:

TIMBRE:
the tonal, color identifier such as bright,
dark, warm, or smoky.

INTONATION:
the unique rise and fall
of someone's vocal pitch.

CADENCE:
the rhythmic flow and modulation.

INFLECTION:
the bend, fold, or turn that shifts
the voice from a monotone course.

If you want dialogue to feel authentic, strive to incorporate the elements above. Look for examples in the books you read.

For example, in the opening scene of *Charlotte's Web*, Fern learns that her father is headed to the hog house to do away with a baby piglet. Fern is outraged and her dialogue reflects it.

"Do *away* with it?" shrieked Fern. "You mean *kill* it? Just because it's smaller than the others?"

The timbre of Fern's shriek comes across as shrill. We feel the rise and fall of her intonation through the use of italics, which also gives her words a feeling of acceleration.

Although reading provides endless examples of crafted dialogue, there's another way to study elements such as timbre and cadence—through active listening.

While I was growing up, my parents frequented an Italian restaurant in the Eastern Market area of Detroit. It was a storied locale, rumored as a preferred venue for mob inaugurations. As a child, I loved the restaurant. It was a fantastic setting, rife with mystery and gin. But the garlic-infused dinners routinely clocked in at over three hours. So I'd pass the time by playing an eavesdropping game.

While fiddling with my fork and staring at the red tablecloth, I'd tune my ear to one of the tables nearby. As the diners spoke, I'd listen to the conversation and try to guess what the people looked like. No one suspected that the kid in pigtails and patent leather shoes was picking up every word. There were generally three tables within earshot:

TABLE 1:

"I says to him, listen, guy,
we can settle this right here, right now."

TABLE 2:

"It makes you uncomfortable?
But, Donald . . . you used to love it like that."

TABLE 3:

"Gino's sister brought it back from Acapulco.
Honey, it was awful . . ."

I could hear their words but couldn't always see the person speaking. Most of the time I'd just eavesdrop, but if the dinner extended with rounds of port and coffee, I'd pass the time by inventing characters and a plot, and then continue the dialogue in my head.

In the car on the way home, I'd inform my family about the scabies from Acapulco that resembled diaper rash, the wiseguy solution with a tire iron, and Donald who no longer felt comfortable with Eileen's boudoir choices.

"It's impolite to eavesdrop," my ever-respectful father would say.

"Wait. Donald said *what* to Eileen?" my ever-intrigued mother would gasp.

I could imitate the conversations because I'd noted the

speed at which they spoke, the filler words they preferred such as *um* or *you know*, and the dynamics of the conversation. I heard the dialogue as a musical score. The alcohol-inspired crescendos were rarely as interesting as the hushed exchanges. But listening closely helped tune my ear to the fluidity and personality of speech. That fluidity is essential.

Dialogue that reads like recitation, flat and robotic, will leave the reader flat and emotionless. So when you're drafting dialogue, it's helpful to turn off your mind and instead turn to your ear.

Think back a bit:

That blowhard bully you once knew—how did they speak?

Think of your parents and grandparents—can you imitate any of their phrasing?

Try to recall the cadence of an old teacher, a boss, or a mentor. Did they have catchphrases or discourse fillers that they relied upon? Did they ever use—or misuse—a term in a memorable way? Imagine this:

The scene is a corporate conference room. Tense. A nervous division manager paces, sweating. He stops and makes a desperate appeal to employees. He says, "Guys, look. I'm not trying to proctologize here. You know that's not my thing. But it's crucial you understand the stakes at play."

The jittery manager had rehearsed and given deep consideration to the meeting. What he thought he was conveying was that he didn't want to *proselytize*—an attempt to convert someone from their beliefs. But what he said, over and over, was *proctologize*, which is not a word at all but might vaguely refer to the rectum. What would have been a forgettable meeting became an unforgettable monologue.

These speech patterns and rhythms include earnest errors and Freudian slips known as *parapraxes*—and they all create authentic dialogue. They can make characters authentic and memorable as well.

And it's important to note that dialogue is not only the words but also the nonverbal expressions *between* the words. The quiet pause, the hike of an eyebrow, the kneading of the hands, or the distracted look the other way. Gestures speak and breathe. And you want them to. They add dynamics that infuse life into the text. They will work for you when writing dialogue.

EXAMPLE #1
"Sure, Mom would really love that," said Jim.

EXAMPLE #2
"Sure," said Jim, biting back a smirk,
"Mom would really love that."

Sometimes, injecting an expression or descriptor between the words makes all the difference. In the first example, Jim appears sincere. In the second, his smirk conveys sarcasm without having to tell the reader "said Jim, sarcastically." Gestures and expressions might also indicate plot enhancers or conflict layers. A slippery grin—is Jim setting his sibling up for failure? Can we trust Jim?

Hopefully not. That makes characters more interesting.

Think back to the Jims in your life. Have you ever known someone who says one thing but means another? Known someone who tries to express themselves but blunders and conveys something entirely different? Have you ever known someone who tries to appear earnest in dialogue but is really making fun of you?

If so, how did they express that?

During a period when I was carrying a few extra pounds, I arrived at a red-carpet event in Hollywood and ran into a journalist I knew.

"Ruta, darling!" She kissed the air near my cheek and her gaze traveled my frame. Her red lips pinched. "My, you're looking so . . . well rested. And boldly wrapped in green silk. Green's a challenging color, isn't it?"

Dialogue is not only *what* someone is saying, but *how* they're saying it, and also what they're *not* saying.

Her "darling," her empty air-kiss, and her lips the color of murder—my "friend" was about as welcoming as a handful of nails scattered in a parking lot.

As you write dialogue, note the movements, the pauses, the flit of the eyes, or the shift in dynamics. Make use of punctuation. When used very sparingly, the em dash, an exclamation point, or an ellipsis can guide the rhythm of your dialogue.

"My, you're looking so . . . well rested."

In the sentence above, the ellipsis conveys the woman is searching for the words she wants to use. The brief pause emphasizes the punch of insult.

Read your dialogue aloud and make certain it sounds true to age. I've seen manuscripts where a child sounds too mature or an adult sounds like a child. If you're writing a historical piece, research the vernacular and, if possible, listen to old radio programs from the region and time period to capture the correct tone, signature style, and poetry of phrasing.

Speaking of phrasing, certain professions contain dialogue with a signature style and tone—the surgeon, the funeral director, the car salesperson, the flight attendant. Can you think of others? My friends with supernatural occupations amaze me with their command of dialogue: The medium once brought through my Lithuanian grandmother with her exact speech pattern and private jokes. The channeler leaves me voicemails from a husky dead doctor advising on sciatica. Bizarre? Definitely. But I listen. It's all research and ear training.

Next time you have the opportunity, dig out old video footage you might have lying around. Listen to the voices. Watch the hand gestures, the facial movements, and the body rhythms that accompany the dialogue. Movement helps animate the scene.

> *Ten-Ten kicked the metal chair into position and*
> *sat down. She flicked me a nod.*
> *"Hey, Snow."*

If you're using memories to write a fictional piece, it's the spirit and tone of a recalled exchange that you'll pull from. Blend the feeling or setting of the recollection with invented conversation so the dialogue doesn't represent a specific person or a single memory. Perhaps you once got into an argument with Uncle Ron in a shoe store. Your fictional characters can absolutely argue in a shoe store, but their words should be their own, not Uncle Ron's.

If you *are* writing about your own personal experience, take care when putting words in other people's mouths. At its best, writing facilitates reflection and comprehension, not condemnation.

And finally, think back to conversations in your life that were memorable. Jot them down and try to insert the dynamics and flow exactly as you remember them.

Examining the dialogue now, with a buffer of time or from a slightly different altitude, you might discover hidden elements of the conversation that slipped by you in the past. Or perhaps your position has evolved? As years pass and your life story progresses, roles sometimes reverse. Child becomes parent and teacher becomes student. When reflecting on dialogue from your past, what conversations stand out most vibrantly in your memory? Are there specific settings and characters associated with the conversations?

When and why, if ever, could it be helpful to return to old conversations and reflect upon them?

Newer Every Day

March 2021

Dear Dad,

I'm working on the dialogue section of the book, asking readers to reflect on memorable conversations. As I'm writing, I'm reflecting on my own cache of memories. And suddenly, old discussions are pushing in. The chats feel so close, I could almost pick them off a tree.

Shiny. Ripe. Not so ripe. Worms. *Pick me!* So many to choose from.

But the ones that call to me, that return to me so often, are the ones with you.

Our perspectives are different, of course. Some conversations might not be memorable for you. And in some cases, my point of view was that of a young girl. Is that a reliable lens?

Youth. Emotional truth. I think it's a pure lens. A lens that sometimes holds a curious inventory of conversations.

"Who cares if they make fun of you?" said

Mom. "Sure, you're a duckling now. But just you wait," she said, pointing her cigarette at me. "They'll lose their chins and you'll look fabulous in a turban."

A Halston turban? That was her balm for bullying? I was seven. But I still recall the conversation. I don't know if you remember, but we laughed, Dad. You were detouring through the kitchen with your black briefcase on the way to work.

"You're not a duckling. You're a swan," you told me. "All children are beautiful."

You'd often say that.

At the time, I found that suspect, but now I couldn't agree more. All children *are* beautiful. And so is your lens, I might add, to have pointed that out. I remember that conversation so clearly.

Here's what else I remember.

How much you loved your job and your work setting. Yes, you're retired now, but back then you were nearing the height of your career in commercial art. Your graphic design studio pulsed like a fabulous creative hive. There were artists, illustrators, photographers, retouchers, typographers, and airbrush wizards using nickel-plated pens that hissed like snakes. Amazing! Your creative teams listened to music, lit candles, took off their shoes, and smoked while they worked. A bookie named Wheels stopped by weekly to collect game bets. Do you remember Wheels, Dad?

You often praised your sales team. I never met them as they were rarely in the office.

"Out drinking with clients," Mom would whisper. "They're all drunks."

"Now, that's not nice. Nor is it true," you'd insist.

Partially true? I recall a voicemail that Mom left about the sales rep who urinated on himself and then passed out. At his desk. At 2:00 p.m.

Your office was always so fun. Sometimes you'd take me with you on weekends.

And you know what I recall vividly? The reception area. The welcoming visual as you walked through the entrance was a black wall with an arching supergraphic. A disco rainbow in yellow, green, and white. Reception was the domain of Bobbi, who handled the phones and greeted clients. Bobbi's white lacquer desk was flanked by chrome-potted plants and diamond-shaped chairs.

"Good afternoon, Sepetys & Associates," she'd say. Her tone was smooth but bright. I practiced it. Maybe one day you'd need an understudy.

If approved, guests would be escorted by Bobbi through a door in the black wall to enter the creative laboratory. But on weekends, Bobbi wasn't there, so I escorted myself. I'd wander the halls and peek through the glass enclosure of each studio, making note of who had the largest selection of markers I might smell. Each space felt unique, intriguing. Some were chromatic, others had cork walls with illustrations. Some were messy with stacks of Pantone color books, spray cans of Krylon acrylic, sheets of Letraset, and leaking jars of rubber cement. And of course there was the windowless security studio where the top secret ad campaigns were sketched.

Lining the company hallways were examples of the firm's popular designs displayed in sleek black frames.

And at the very end of the hall, behind an open door awash with light, was your office, Dad. But let's admit it. Unlike the fun factory corridors, your office had a distinctly different feel.

"Well, hello, dolly," you'd always say, smiling, and wave me in.

Two iconic Pollock chairs were positioned in front of your long glass desk. It felt very official to sit in them. Yes, you're right, you still have the very same desk and chairs.

The soft sound of smooth jazz floated from your radio whose dial enjoyed a permanent residency on WJZZ. Your office at the studio was lovely and elegant but lacked the whimsical feel of the others. It was different.

You were different.

You wore suits and pressed shirts with monogrammed sleeves. You shined your shoes each morning and never removed them in the office. And unlike the artist pods that all contained highly personal items, your office didn't have any items that pertained to your own story or history. Was that intentional?

When you left on Thursdays, did they know you were heading out with your soccer team? Did they know you spoke Lithuanian and German? Did they know you cut the grass on Fridays and drove me to mime class on Saturdays? I wasn't sure people knew.

"So, what's the plan for today?" you'd ask as I'd spin in the chair.

"Um, can I have some markers?"

"May I have some markers?" you'd tease. "Yes, you may."

We walked down the hall and I stopped at an open door. "This one has the largest box," I said.

"Oh, it's not a box," you explained. "It's called a taboret. And that's someone's personal office. We'll get you some markers from the production room."

I stared longingly at the massive display of markers through the glass wall. The production room was cool, too, but there had to be more than a hundred markers. Right here.

You patted my shoulder. "These spaces

belong to the talent. They're private. You understand."

I nodded. I did understand. You were always respectful. The kids in our neighborhood had a nickname for you—the Politeness Man. Did you know that?

"Why do some of the men have long hair?" I asked on our way to the production room.

"They're artists," you said.

"You're an artist. You went to art school."

"Yes, I'm artistic. But I'm more interested in business. True artists need to explore and express their ideas regardless of where they might lead. They're more inspired to create art than market it."

Although I didn't grasp the idea during the conversation, that was my first introduction to the concept of artists and artistic creative workers.

Yes, you were an artist. But you were more driven as a creative worker. You had to be.

As a refugee, you had once lost everything— your extended family, your country—but you regrouped and rebuilt. To you, anything was possible, even creative pursuits, but you had to have a plan. Remember?

Your leaps were netless. Everything was a grand adventure. "Believe it" was your mantra. You did. So we did, too.

And aging—it never concerned you, Dad.

Tucked alongside your desk calendar was your favorite quote from Emily Dickinson: *We turn not older with years, but newer every day.*

Now, looking at it from a different altitude, it was incredible. You didn't fear failure, you didn't fear bankruptcy, and you didn't fear aging. You became newer every day. And you encouraged us to do the same.

"A second mortgage?!" shrieked Mother. (Oh boy, remember that?) "Aren't you afraid we'll lose the house?" she bellowed.

"No. I have a plan," you responded calmly.

You always had a plan. And if the ground shifted, you'd regroup and create another plan. Suit by day, soccer by night. Broken bones, head injuries, knee surgeries, and a heart attack on the playing field. And up from the rubble you'd rise, better and newer than before, and always in time to attend every school event or recital.

When I graduated from college, I sought counsel at your desk. I remember the conversation.

"I want to be a rock 'n' roll manager and move to Los Angeles," I blurted.

"Great! What's your plan?" you asked, reaching for the yellow legal pad. "You'll need a business plan for yourself and one for each of your clients. Draft a plan that covers ten years. You'll have to work very hard, but you can absolutely do this. Believe it."

Believe it? What father with an ounce of sanity would encourage his youngest daughter to set out into the cesspool of rock 'n' roll with a business plan but no money, no contacts, and no experience?

But those two words, faithful residents within your dialogue, meant that you not only believed it was possible; you believed it was possible for me. You believed in me before I believed in me. Yes, you did, Dad. Except the mime class. You said that was bullshit.

Time passed and, of course, you were right, it does take ten years. And there were countless discussions along the way. Our planning summits and coaching conversations continued through my departures from Michigan and Los Angeles, my move to Nashville, and even to my transition to writing. Yes, of course I remember what you told me.

"Writing books. Great! You can do this."

In the meantime, you built businesses, consulted for others, played soccer until you were seventy-five, and reluctantly announced your business retirement at eighty-one. The diagnosis came at eighty-three.

Yes, you were eighty-three.

You were in the exam room. I was standing in the hall with the doctor.

"Ruta, I know your father's an athlete. New studies show that in some cases, this condition might be linked to athletic injuries. Has your dad sustained many injuries?"

Athletic injuries?

I suddenly heard Mom's voice, calling the martini-drinking doctor.

"Hi, Cal. Do you have time for some stitches tonight?"

Athletic injuries?

"Hi, love, it's me. Remember when your father was in a full-body cast . . ."

Athletic injuries?

That story . . . your head. Amnesia.

I swallowed past the lump forming in my throat. "Yes," I nodded. "Athletic injuries."

You? You were totally unconcerned. Your dialogue was so *you*.

"Look, guys, I'm eighty-three, I have arthritis and spinal stenosis, too. We all have something to deal with," you said.

We created a plan. We pushed onward.

You changed nothing. You went golfing. You went Jet-Skiing. You rocked the elliptical several times per week. You cried for three years straight after losing Mom. You continued to live wholeheartedly.

"When were you diagnosed?" the instructor asked during a boxing class.

"Forgive me, diagnosed with what?" you replied with all sincerity. I leaned over and whispered, reminding you. "Oh, that. That's nothing. Believe it."

You truly believed it. You pushed on.

Things became more difficult. You pushed on.

We had a plan. And I remember the day it occurred to me that we might actually need it. We were sitting in the neurologist's office for a routine appointment. You looked at me, suddenly concerned. "Who helps my sister with her author business? Does she have an agent or a manager to help with her books and tours?"

Your sister? No, I'm . . .

Oh.

It was at that moment that I understood. Our dialogue paradigm—it was changing.

I smiled and put my hand on yours.

"She's well taken care of, Dad. She has an excellent team and a great plan."

Your shoulders exhaled. "Good. I'm so relieved."

Our conversations have shifted now. Medication, balance therapy, and many appointments with specialists. Plans are being rewritten, and, to jog your memory, I read this letter of reminiscences to you, sometimes daily.

But despite your condition, I want to assure you of something, Dad. You're living as you've always lived —mightily. You're still a fearless dragon slayer. I know you'd take comfort in that, just as I take comfort in the memories of our dialogue. Sometimes it helps to write about it. Like this.

"It's getting better. I'll be better tomorrow," you tell me.

You believe it. You truly believe it. And each time I'm certain you've stepped over the cognitive threshold to become a warrior of windmills, up from the rubble you'll rise. My phone will ring at 6:00 a.m. with DAD illuminating the screen. Is it the nurse?

"Hi, dolly. So . . . is Ensure something athletes drink? Or just old people?"

Wow, there you are. There you are. I try to control my joy.

"Ensure, yes, that's part of the plan," I remind you. That always makes you feel better.

At this point, there's not much planning to do. If the fates allow, I'll be with you as you whisper out, just as you and Mom were with me as I came screaming in. But in the meantime, soldier on, Dad. You're doing the only thing you know how to do. And we love you for it.

Yes, on some days it's difficult to recall what things used to be like. You're different. But that doesn't matter, because I take comfort in the memory of our past conversations and the words you truly loved, because now, they apply more than ever:

We turn not older with years, but newer every day.

Dialogue and Memory

THERE ARE CONVERSATIONS WE REMEMBER.

Conversations we wish we could forget.

Some conversations we never got to have.

It's all dialogue.

The conversations live a world away, yet at the same time, exist under our skin. How can that be possible and how can we best access them?

Sometimes, to open a door to the landscape of memory, it's helpful to write things in epistolary form—to ourselves or others. In the previous section, I use the letter exercise to unearth memories and dialogue not only for myself but also for my beloved father whose mind and memory have been stolen. To prompt recollection of the dialogue, I return to his favorite setting and allow the sensory details to surround me. It's there, in the world of commercial design, that I feel and hear him most clearly.

Is there a setting or time period where you might recall dialogue more clearly? Where does your memory live amid that actual dialogue? Is it internal dialogue, conversations you wish you'd had, or conversations you actually had?

You.

Try using your own perspective first. Yes, others may have

been there. They have their own point of view. In the previous example of conversations with my father, I don't include comments or dialogue from my siblings. They are my best friends and trusted confidants. They are probably even closer with Dad than I am.

But remember, memory is selective.

They have their own memories and perspective. They have their own stories to tell.

Often, the way memories linger within us might relate in some way to our own identity construction. That path of memory is rich, yet slippery. There might be patches of black ice or buckled ground. Writer, poet, and philosopher Jorge Luis Borges captured it this way: "We are our memory, we are that chimerical museum of shifting shapes, that pile of broken mirrors."

When writing fiction, we can absolutely fuse and weave together multiple pieces, shapes, and memories to invent dialogue. But when writing autobiography or documenting a family story, take care with the words. Remember, we've all made mistakes. In the universe of memories, we're all the villain in someone's story. If they were writing about us, how would we hope they'd express the events and dialogue exchanged? How might they navigate what could be the slippery patches of black ice between memory and emotion?

Memory.

Shifting shapes. Broken mirrors.

Things said and left unsaid. Verbals and nonverbals. External and internal.

It's all a form of dialogue.

DIALOGUE · RECAP

꙰

- One of the best ways to study dialogue is through ear training and active listening.

- As you write, read your dialogue aloud and listen for fluidity. Have others read it aloud as well. How does it sound to you?

- Keep in mind that authentic dialogue sometimes contains errors and imperfect rhythms.

- Ask others to read your dialogue sections and inquire whether they feel true to age.

- Dialogue is not only the words but also what is expressed between the words. Include select nonverbals to show the reader what is happening.

- Remember to describe not only what someone is saying but also *how* they're saying it, as well as what they're not saying.

- Listen and note the cadence and timbre of the voices in your life. How do they speak?

- Think back: What conversations from your past live in your memory most clearly? Why?

- Are there certain settings that evoke memories of conversations? Mentally revisit those settings.

- Take care when putting words in the mouths of others. Speak from your own perspective.

DIALOGUE · WRITING PROMPTS

❧ Think of a conversation that remains in your head and heart. Write dialogue to either archive the conversation or rewrite it as you wish it had occurred.

❧ Look at a photograph of yourself with others or choose a picture from a magazine. Write dialogue for the scene in the photo.

❧ Rewrite the flat dialogue below, injecting nonverbals and elements that might bring it to life. How does it change the conversation? Try rewriting it several times.

"Wait, you did what?" said Todd.

"You heard me," said Kelly.

❧ The car breaks down during a drive. Write a scene of dialogue between the driver and the person they call for help. Try to include the setting and infuse conflict layers and escalating plot obstacles as the dialogue progresses.

Two musicians in a band are discussing what their new album cover should look like. One is an egocentric extrovert who loves attention. The other is an artistic, soft-spoken daydreamer. Write a section of dialogue that captures their conversation about the album cover.

Freudian Slip

An error in speech that might involve the subconscious mind is called a *Freudian slip*, named after psychoanalyst Sigmund Freud. Imagine an unexpected guest arrives at your home. Instead of saying "I'm glad you're here," what comes out of your mouth is "I'm mad you're here." Freud believed these slips of the tongue, also known as *parapraxes*, were communications from the unconscious mind.

Q: Which hair metal band released an album entitled *Slip of the Tongue*? (Just making sure you're still paying attention.)

Bookie

The term *bookie*—short for *bookmaker*—refers to a person who accepts and pays off bets at agreed-upon odds, most often on sporting events. For centuries, the term *bookie* was associated with illegal gambling, but in 2018, the US Supreme Court gave states permission to legalize sports betting. With the recent expansion of betting and online gambling, bookmaking is no longer a criminal operation, but a legitimate and legal profession.

Q: Why is managing bets called *bookmaking*?

Pantone Colors

It's not dark blue or midnight blue, but somewhere in between.

Verbally explaining a color shade is challenging and leaves margin for interpretive error. In 1956, a college graduate hired by two advertising execs devised the Pantone Matching System. The system, known as PMS, was created to help designers and printers specify and control colors for print projects. Each Pantone color is assigned a numeric identifier and use of the specific number will guarantee a color match from project conception to production.

Q: How many Pantone colors are there?

Emily Dickinson

Emily Dickinson, a lyric poet, remains one the most prominent figures in American poetry. Her poems are often short, with melodic qualities touching upon themes of life, death, nature, and immortality. Dickinson wrote of life as she grew to know and experience it, eagerly searching for magic and meaning. Although she was reportedly solitary in nature, her solitude produced a large body of work prior to her death at age fifty-five. The majority of Dickinson's poems do not have titles but are instead referenced by their opening line.

Q: How many poems did Emily Dickinson write and how many were published during her lifetime?

≫RESEARCH≪

Investigation

RESEARCH.

The mere mention of the word causes some to shudder. Especially students. Perhaps it implies spending long hours under fluorescent lights, sitting in front of a screen, or endless note-taking? If you're one of the many who doesn't care for the word, try swapping *research* for *investigation*.

Suddenly, it feels more exciting.

As an author of historical fiction, I know that research is essential to my writing process. But it's also essential for inspiration. Researching a topic inevitably leads to other threads I find fascinating. At times, it feels like the work of a detective—tracking clues, hunting down missing material, traveling to various locations, and interviewing sources.

A wise first step is to determine how to organize and retain your research. There are many options. Some writers use spreadsheets, others digital or paper index cards or documents in a series of labeled folders that live online or on the computer. I do a mix of all of them. When I begin a project, I buy a new blank journal. I save documents and articles on my laptop, but also keep my personal research notes and impressions in the journal. When I finish the book, my journal is essentially a handwritten nonfiction companion to my novel. It's also a repository of memories.

Choose the organizational method that will be the easiest and most reliable for you.

The genre you're working in will determine the type of research necessary. If you're writing a medical thriller and are not well versed in medicine, you'll probably have to do quite a bit of research in order for it to sound authentic. If you're writing fantasy, your worldbuilding might be entirely your own.

IN CONSIDERING YOUR STORY TOPIC, ASK YOURSELF:

What interests me most about this topic?

What don't I know?

What facts am I missing and where might I find them?

Begin by researching what interests you most. That will keep you engaged and motivated to continue.

Research sources are endless. You might consult nonfiction, textbooks, magazines, newspaper archives, photo libraries, government archives, local archives, yearbooks, ancestry websites, social registers, maps, academic papers, journals, memoirs, family archives, cookbooks, social media sites, music archives, and even eBay. In terms of people, you might consult historians, academics, specialists, experts, true witnesses, and their family members.

Take care when using photos for research. Human experience has many angles and it's always prudent to question: What lies outside the frame? Who was behind the lens and what were they trying to capture? What am I not seeing? If there's a photo that's particularly compelling, look for another photo of the same scene but from a different angle.

While researching in a national archive, I came upon a historical photo that was incredibly powerful. It pictured a young boy, holding a weapon larger than his body. His face pulled with fear and his clothes were painted with blood. The narrative of a child soldier emerged in my head. Tragic, horrific. I found another photo of the same scene, but from a different angle. In the second photo the child with the weapon was pictured, but also something else. Hanging in the corner of the frame was a movie camera. The story wasn't of a child soldier, but of a movie shoot.

In looking at the first photo, I had created a false narrative. That's not a concern if you're writing straight fiction, but in writing historical fiction or nonfiction, it's a huge misstep. So take care to find several photos of the same scene.

Once you've done your reading research and acquainted yourself with the topic, you can move on to one of the most exciting parts of research—personal interviews.

Prior to interviewing or speaking with a potential research source, do your homework. Time is a valuable commodity, and if someone is generous enough to share theirs with you, respect that. Research them first. If the person has written something on the topic, read it. If there's something they're passionate about or involved in, look into it. Some people become annoyed if they're asked for general information that already exists elsewhere or has been shared widely. Researching your interview topic beforehand will give you a framework of knowledge and create a more compelling and productive conversation.

If you'd like to record the interview, ask well in advance, at least several days before the meeting or call. It's not fair to put someone on the spot in the moment and say, "Oh, you don't mind if I record this, do you?"

They may mind. So much that they may not proceed with the interview.

When you begin the interview, you'll probably have a list of information or details you're hoping to obtain. But keep in mind that the best information and material are often things we would never think or know to ask. If you're interviewing someone about a specific place, event, or time period, include some sense memory questions—questions that might transport the person back to that moment in an immersive way.

When I was writing *The Fountains of Silence*, I interviewed many people who lived in Spain amid the Franco dictatorship. During the conversations, I would ask questions to open the door of memory:

Imagine you're looking out an open window of your childhood home. Tell me, what do you see? What do you smell? What do you hear?

Suddenly, the descriptions and information I received were well beyond facts and figures. The person might describe the floral patterns on the lace curtains or wallpaper, the scent of paprika, the fog of exhaust from a bus that rumbled by, or perhaps the boot stomp of the militia that produced the chill of a beast at their back.

Tell me about the curtains would not have been a question on my list. But suddenly, I had the information and details. Detail adds authenticity to the setting.

As you research and collect data, write down not only the

facts but also the feelings. Note the emotions you felt when learning the information, or the emotions conveyed by the person who shared the information. You'll want to incorporate that into your writing. If possible, research and work on your manuscript draft during the same period. That way, your writing retains the emotional resonance of the research at the time you experienced it. If there's a lengthy gap between researching and writing, it's sometimes difficult to recall the feelings that were associated with the facts.

And remember to ask questions that create room for more information:

 ❧ What might be
misunderstood about this?
❧ What aspects do you wish people
would focus on more often?
❧ What might others not know
or understand about this?
❧ Is there anyone else you feel
I should speak to?

We often turn to research for investigation, confirmation, or verification. But there's another opportunity I mentioned earlier that's sometimes overlooked: inspiration.

Writers are often asked where we get our ideas for stories. Ideas are everywhere, but recognizing them as story prompts requires a presence and awareness combined with activation of the imagination.

I often visit estate sales. I'll walk through an old home, deciphering stories from the items I see. A dress with a cigarette burn. A telegram of condolence. Dusty trophies. Shoes so worn at the heels that I'm convinced the owner danced herself to death. Every item has a story attached to it.

Sacred texts and personal Bibles are an underestimated research source, but they can be more informative than letters or even a diary. The passages that are underlined, the prayer cards, the notes, dates, and items tucked inside—they all tell a deeply personal story. Sacred books are often a place of safekeeping. I once discovered a Bible at a flea market that had cash and checks tucked inside.

Stories live and breathe everywhere around us.

Your house is full of items and each item contains a story.

Your life is full of happenings and each one is wrapped in story.

Relationships, jobs, journeys, missteps, and mistakes.

Comb through your experiences. Look through a different lens. Walk around a memory, a time period, or a specific event. Interview the memory and jot down questions about it.

Every writer investigates in their own way. So initially, don't worry about structure for your research journal. Research and write about a topic in whatever way helps excavate details attached to the experience.

Over the years, I've developed my own methods to peer into the glass case of history and memory. I'll provide an example of my research musings here so you can see what I mean. As you'll notice, sometimes the glass reflects tears. But more often, it's fogged by laughter at my own reflection.

THE PROCESS OF BUILDING DIMENSIONAL CHARACTERS

(RESEARCH JOURNAL EXCERPT)

RESEARCH TOPIC: Character development
through hope, humiliation, simile,
and juxtaposition.

RESEARCH QUESTIONS: Can rejection
deepen our sense of self? Can intimacy with loneliness
be a positive, instead of a negative? Can failure
provide compost for characters? What role
does juxtaposition play?

MEMORIES TO INTERVIEW:
Dating / Valentine's Day

FEBRUARY—THE FEELING

February is an in-between month. January's promise of a new beginning is fading. We're tired of winter, but spring is still out of reach. Much of the country is cold and gray. Pasty, dry skin. Even worse, February tends to bring out cynicism in people, doesn't it? Yes, the Bitter Bettys are out in full force in February, doubting and naysaying to the extreme. Beware the lurking Bitter Betty. If you're not careful, she'll have you by the ankles, dragging you under to the miserable kingdom, where nothing is possible and things will never get better. Ever. It's a very dangerous place.

INTERROGATING CYNICISM

But what makes us cynical? I'd like to research this. Is it low expectations? Habits of self-limitation? Or maybe just plain fear of disappointment? Many writers have degrees in disappointment, don't we? Let's not forget those instructive H's of heartbreak, hope, hilarity, and humiliation. After all, experiencing the lowest of lows provides a frame of reference to appreciate moments of happiness. Discouragements also help us create dimensional characters others can relate to. I believe in disappointment as a motivating, illuminating force. Get your heart dirty. In fact, how about taking a whirl at feeling like a loser? Check! Or perhaps publicly embarrassed? Done that, too. In my experience, Valentine's Day and dating is a great place to start.

DATING RESEARCH

When are most teens allowed to date? The hard rule in our house was sixteen. And of course, each of my parents had different gender-presumptive parameters for suitors than I did.

Dad: "Is he Lithuanian? Where did he go to school? What's his plan?"

Mom: "What are his teeth like? Is he a bragger? He doesn't wear nasty cologne, does he?"

But what if dating were considered research? An amusing study to create characters and stories. If that were the case, I have over twenty years of solid research. Enough to write an entire series of books about my hundreds of disastrous and fabulous dating adventures. They could easily be transformed into characters, plots, conflict layers, and studies of archetypes.

IMAGINE THESE CHARACTERS:

The Hungarian diesel breather who insisted on
calling me Gruta because it made him feel safer.

The pilot who wasn't really a pilot. (Scary.)
The convict who really *was* a convict.
(Not as scary as the fake pilot.)

The passenger in the Venice train station—
a weeklong divine date across three countries.

The hilarious wedding crasher who
taught me how to be a wedding crasher.

The soap opera actor who dreamed
of being a dry cleaner.

The concerned prosecutor who gave me a
laminated GET OUT OF JAIL FREE card. Literally.

The judgy academic who requested my
ACT score and then never returned from the bathroom.

The Gulf War vet with full-body tattoos
and a car horn that played twelve American tunes.

The beautiful boy with the leaky bladder
who helped me escape from a convent.

Oh. Is that ten already? They came in such a flurry. And they're not even the top ten. I have so many more. Each a lesson in humility. Each a full plot, setting, and story of their own. But I'm saving those for future Februarys. Heavy artillery against the Bitter Bettys.

Do others have dating misadventure memories they can use as research? I wonder.

RELATIONSHIPS IN SIMILE

Consider using past relationships as a study of descriptive simile to identify facts and valuable conclusions:

> **FACT:** *Kissing him was like eating dry pasta.*
> *Research conclusion: He wasn't "the one."*

> **FACT:** *He said the date felt a bit like a sinus infection.*

Research conclusion: I don't think he'll call.

FACT: *I laughed so hard, I wet my pants.*
(Nope. No simile.)
Research conclusion: Marry the wedding crasher.

VALENTINE'S DOOMSDAY MEMORIES

Reaching into my memory bank to dig out some of my Valentine's Day disasters:

THE YEAR OF THE WITCH

In elementary school each class had a Valentine's Day party. We taped small paper bags to the backs of our chairs and circulated around the room, dropping petite envelopes with valentines in each sack. Then we returned to our seats and ate cupcakes and other treats while reading our stacks of cards. A few weeks earlier, a small bump had sprouted on my chin. Imagine my complete mortification when my grandmother announced, "It'z a wart. Get me za vodka and a knife."

Fortunately, my parents decided to take me to a dermatologist rather than let Granny carve me up. The appointment, however, was a few days *after* Valentine's Day. I wanted to wear a Band-Aid on my face, but my parents assured me it wasn't necessary.

"No one will notice. You can barely see it. All children are beautiful . . ."

Well, I was so excited to tear into that bag of valentines hanging from my chair. I had seen the class cutie putting names on his valentines in green marker. I quickly sifted through my small envelopes and found the one labeled *Ruta* in green. My heart fluttered. I had chosen a special valentine for Class Cutie, one with a glittery moon and stars on it. Maybe he had chosen something special for me, something I could show my best girlfriend and squeal about?

I opened the envelope. The valentine had a picture of Scooby-Doo on it. Written in green ink under Scooby was: *To witchy wart face.*

I looked over at Class Cutie. He was sitting with his friends. They all laughed and pointed at me.

Total. Complete. Devastation.

Holy humiliation.

Deep cut. In elementary school.

I immediately faked a huge laugh and nodded at the boys.

Their faces quirked with confusion.

I put the valentine back in the bag and swallowed a bite of cupcake past the lump in my throat. On the way home from school I threw the valentine in the bushes because I knew my parents would be sad if they saw it.

That was the day I learned the hard truth.

To other children, not all children are beautiful.

FRUIT COCKTAIL AND A FAST CAR

There was also the fantastic Valentine's dinner—by myself. When I lived in Los Angeles, the guy I was seeing suggested we meet at a hip beachfront restaurant in Santa Monica for Valentine's Day. I eagerly made the reservation and paid in advance as required. I arrived early and sat at the table alone, watching others popping bottles of champagne and tangling their feet together under the table. After ninety minutes I got the hint and went home. I received a message from a friend who saw my "boyfriend" with someone else. I stood at the kitchen sink in my black dress eating canned fruit cocktail and listening to the same song, over and over, on repeat.

You got a fast car, I want a ticket to anywhere.

WELCOME TO PARADISE

Let's not forget the year that I nearly worked myself to death on a music tour and the doctor suggested I take a break. I cashed in all my flight miles and flew to the South Pacific around Valentine's Day. Alone. People were convinced I was a widow and showered me with pity, tropical drinks, and discount coupons to visit a vanilla farm.

Wow, aren't these all fabulously miserable?

RESEARCH CONCLUSIONS

Vulnerability presents possibility.

Rejection might be protection.

Failure leads to wisdom.

I'm grateful to know what it's like to have my heart fall in the mud, to be humiliated, to be sitting alone at a restaurant while diners send pathetic glances my way. It's all research. It's experiencing all that life has to offer. Deeply and fully. That means living amid—and through—the juxtapositions.

THE TENSION OF JUXTAPOSITION

Strong writing incorporates juxtaposition, the enhancing contrast of different elements by placing them together on the page. And writers need to look for those juxtapositions during research. War and peace. Love and loss. Strength through struggle. Beauty and horror. Opposing elements chafe and create sparks. Each becomes more powerful as they illuminate the other. Such is the case with human interaction, and this explains why the cliché "opposites attract" is used so often.

What topic or experience from your past could you research more deeply? Could you investigate your memories through metaphor, or jot random recollections in a research journal? While recording your research and data, make note of the emotions peeking through. Reflect and determine what those emotions might tell you.

These dating stories as research may sound horrible. But they're an interesting study of human interaction and juxtaposition. They also present the conclusion that repeated attempts and repeated failures eventually yield wisdom and reward. Imagine how the heavens break open when a gorgeous wedding crasher walks into the world of a bookish introvert.

Suddenly, life is grand.

And love, it gives you courage and wings.

Happy February!

Beat away the Bitter Bettys.

Use a broom if you have to.

RESEARCH · RECAP

- Think of research as investigation or detective work.

- Choose a system to organize and retain your research.

- Begin your research with what interests you most.

- When looking at photos, ask yourself: What lies outside the frame? Is there another angle?

- Before an interview, make sure to research the person extensively.

- If you'd like to record an interview, request permission well in advance.

- When interviewing someone about a past event, consider including sense memory questions.

- As you're researching, make note of your own feelings and emotions.

- Research for inspiration! Conduct your own research adventures.

- Revisit a memory and jot down research questions about it. What would you like to know?

- Interrogate your cynicism. What is making you cynical about something?

- Choose an element from your personal history, school experience, or relationship experience. Create a research journal entry about it.

- Identify juxtaposition in your research and use it to illuminate elements of the story.

- To bring the story to life, infuse the emotions you noted during your research into your writing.

- The Uncover and Discover portions of this book—have you realized? They're actually sneaky research prompts!

RESEARCH · WRITING PROMPTS

❧ If you were going to fake being a pilot, what sort of research would you have to do? Jot down a list. Do some quick investigation. Write a paragraph of dialogue as a fake pilot.

❧ You have a seven-hour layover in Venice, Italy, while traveling. What sort of advance research would you do to occupy your time during the seven hours? Write for ten minutes about your fictional layover.

❧ Think of someone, anyone, you're curious to know more about. Research and determine: What city were they born in? What was the weather like in that city on the date of their birth?

❧ Take a trip to a local thrift shop. Find a book or an item that has someone's name on it. Put your detective cap on and research to determine what sort of information you can gather about that person. How much can you find?

❧ Create a story about the life and journey of the item from the thrift shop.

- You have the opportunity to interview anyone of your choice, living or dead. Draft five interview questions for that person.

- Think back to past relationships—platonic, family, or romantic. List details and personality traits you remember. Could any become fictional characters?

Estate Sales

Most estate sales differ from garage and yard sales by this fact: the people selling the items are often unrelated to the family who owned them. For a fee, the estate sale coordinator provides services and takes on the responsibility of organizing and lifting the burden of memory and, in many cases, the burden of "stuff" from the family. In addition to being full of story and history, estate sales present the opportunity to find hidden treasures.

Q: What are some of the most valuable items ever discovered at an estate sale?

The Persian Gulf War

In 1990, Iraqi president Saddam Hussein attempted to take over the State of Kuwait, a country in the Middle East. The invasion led to an air and ground war led by the United States and supported by coalition forces that included over thirty nations. The operations were code-named Operation Desert Shield and Operation Desert Storm and took place from August of 1990 to February of 1991. It's estimated that more than 650,000 American service members served on active duty during the conflict.

Q: What was at stake during the Gulf War and what was the outcome?

Valentine

Although Valentine's Day is supposed to represent love and romance, you might be hard-pressed to find a legitimate historical connection to the candy and cupids that define the holiday as many of us know it. In fact, there's a chance that Valentine's Day dates to the Romans in the third century, when Emperor Claudius II executed two men named Valentine in separate years on February 14. Not sure if red roses were sent.

Q: Who was St. Valentine?

Vanilla Farms

Today, the vast majority of foods are produced with vanilla flavoring, not natural vanilla beans. Vanilla grows best in tropical climates and is labor-intensive to produce. Vanilla plants grow as climbing orchids and the pod, referred to as the vanilla bean, is picked unripe, submerged in hot water, and then laid out to dry for a lengthy period of time. Each pod contains thousands of tiny aromatic and flavorful seeds. The majority of today's vanilla comes from Madagascar, the island of Réunion, Tahiti, and Mexico.

Q: Natural vanilla is the second most expensive spice. What's the first?

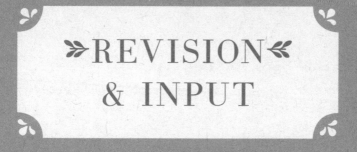

REVISION
& INPUT

The Tenth Draft

DO NOT SKIP THIS CHAPTER.

It should have been the first chapter of the book.

Revision.

It's that important.

Ideas are so elusive that when we actually manage to get them down on the page, the experience is either so seductive, tiring, or both that we're often eager to immediately share them, submit them, or publish them.

Share them? Yes.

Submit them? Not yet.

As many before me have said, writing is rewriting. Yes, there are those rare few whose first drafts are pure brilliance, but that's not the norm. Many of us struggle to get something, anything, on the page in the first place. Some of us are so consumed with fear we can't get a word down.

And that's entirely normal.

Writer's block is fear. Fear that it won't be good enough, fear that we're not good enough, fear that we have no right to call ourselves writers, fear that others will hate it, fear that we'll never write something worthwhile, fear that maybe we're not worthwhile, fear that we'll never know how to proceed with the draft we have.

Fear.

In the early stages, it's essential to give yourself the courage to fail. And to do that, you must accept this tried-and-true draft method:

Write crap.

Yes.

Give yourself permission to write crap. Absolute crap. Assure yourself over and over:

It's just a draft. Yes, it's crap, but this isn't final. Just a draft.

And as you write, there may be elements that remain, but the true form will emerge in revision. You must revise. Revision is a gift.

If you are a performer, an athlete, or a competitor of some sort, imagine being able to go back and change something about your performance. Those changes—they might make all the difference. They might transform a losing game into a spectacular, winning game.

But the tendency is to rush. And please understand, that's natural. We're excited.

Look! I have a chapter! Look! I have a draft!

We feel we don't need an editor or additional eyes on it. Part of that is excitement. And part of that is because we don't want to hear that it might need more work.

But it does. It always does. It needs revision.

If you put the work aside for a period of time and come back to it with fresh eyes, you'll see things you missed, you'll identify clunky rhythms and awkward sentence structure. You'll catch errors. If there's someone who knows you well, someone you trust, ask them to read your draft and give you some input.

I've been part of the same writing group for nearly twenty years. They see my pages before my agent, before my editor, before anyone. There are five of us in the group, so I receive independent feedback from four separate people. And that's indescribably valuable.

Yes, sometimes it hurts. My group is very tough on me, and I'll admit there have been times after receiving their input that I've stomped, cried, and pouted for days. I was once so bereft after a group critique that I inhaled an entire box of Pepperidge Farm cookies. No, not a pouch of Milano cookies; the big box. I ate an entire Entertaining Collection. Forty-two cookies in one sitting—a grand pity party—and it all went down so easily.

My writing group had said my pages needed more work. I should have listened to them. But instead, I took the manuscript to a national writing conference and submitted it for evaluation. I felt certain that a professional would see its merit. The editor who critiqued my work was indeed professional—an editorial VP of the largest publishing house at the time. The editor asked me about my inspirations, my goals, and whether I was committed to growing as a writer.

"Yes, of course," I gushed. "Please don't sugarcoat anything. I'm here to learn."

Our rapport felt instant. This was promising.

"Excellent," replied the editor. "You seem hardworking and very open. If you stick with it, you'll eventually find your way. But what you've submitted is obnoxious, annoying, and your narrative voice is grating. To be honest, jury duty holds more appeal than these pages."

✳ ✳ ✳

Have you ever experienced the hot splotch of shame and embarrassment crawling up your neck? Have you ever pretended to be invested in the conversation at hand, when you were actually dying inside?

My writing group had told me—plainly and sensitively—that the work was flawed. But instead of accepting it and believing them, I spent good money to present bad pages to an editor.

I cringe thinking of it. But when I finally opened myself to revision and change, things began to fall into place. I soon realized that I was writing in the wrong genre altogether. What a gift. An epiphany I'm convinced arrived because I was open to receive it.

It bruises our ego to hear our work isn't perfect, that the characters aren't realistic, or that we've missed the mark. It's hard enough to write in the first place; do we have to rewrite?

Yes. We do.

The concept or story might be fully formed in our minds, especially if it's inspired from a memory or a personal experience. But because it's familiar to us, we might assume others will understand it, too. Receiving input on our work gives us a view from the outside in. It identifies sections that might be unclear. It also gives us a view of how readers, booksellers, and the media might see it. That's valuable.

After my manuscript goes through the meat grinder of my writing group, I take a breath. I try to reflect on the input, rather than react to it. A breather and a period of reflection is essential because our egoic self and our vulnerable self are often the first line of defense. Sometimes our psyche processes criticism like this:

The book isn't perfect. →
I'm not perfect. → Maybe I'm terrible. →
I can't be a writer.

The book isn't perfect. →
They don't get me. → No one gets me. →
Screw them all.

The book isn't perfect. →
I don't know how to make it better. → I give up.

Perfect. Perfect. As I said in the introduction, anyone who tells you that their life is perfection is either lying—or dreadfully boring. Perfection is a curated world of compare and despair. It's entirely forgettable. No, we are not perfect. But we are perfect in our imperfection. It's our imperfections of character, dialogue, and perspective that make us interesting and memorable. So try to process like this:

The book isn't perfect. → Of course not. →
It's just a draft!

I'm not perfect. → Of course not. →
Hooray!

Writing well requires patience and a commitment to constant improvement. Once you embark upon the path toward publication, you'll go through multiple rounds of revisions and copyedits, so it's best to learn the skill of revision early to avoid rookie mistakes of impatience.

When you revise, don't aim to make your manuscript perfect. Aim to make it memorable. What will leave the story lingering in readers' minds or inspire them to tell others about it? I put my full drafts through at least ten revisions. And my editors will attest that often I'm still trying to revise after the book is turned in. I share it with research partners, educators, and others I trust for feedback.

Working in music for over twenty years taught me a bit about feedback.

I watched my mentors—brilliant artists and songwriters—get sliced to shreds by reviewers. And when it happened, some of their peers feigned shock but secretly gloated. The record companies shrank into the shadows, whispering with concern that the review tarnished the artists and made them uncool.

But my mentors? They processed the input. They asked important questions that gave immediate context and cut to the chase:

Who is allowed to steal my joy? → No one.

Who do I love and who loves me? →
Loyal inner circle.

Is a corporation capable of love? → No.

One of my mentors sent champagne to a ripper reviewer. Another wrote a hit song with the defiant refrain that no one can steal your hope unless you let them. And I return often to one of my favorite lyric reminders that captures the crushing view from the bottom—*hey, you can't "brake" the broken.*

They shook it off. They laughed. They moved on. They continued to create music. They won Grammys, Lifetime Achievement Awards, Billboard Music Awards, and inductions into the Hall of Fame.

I watched and learned. A review doesn't speak for you. But a catalog of work does.

And to build a catalog of work takes time. It takes finding your voice, writing and rewriting, processing input, and understanding that revision and change are part of the growth process.

Please remember that it's not just our manuscript that's a work in progress.

We're all a work in progress.

May I Tell You Something?

❧

THE VALET TAKES MY CAR AND disappears down San Vicente Boulevard. I wrestle with the decision. I can't afford valet parking, but I can't afford to be late for lunch. I walk into the restaurant and a sentry of a hostess dressed in black hikes an eyebrow. She quickly steps forward to block my path.

"May I help you?"

I give her the name. His name.

"Oh, of course. Follow me, please."

I follow her through the narrow path between tables, trying not to notice the well-known actress, the Olympic gold medalist, and the member of a boy band who's much too young to be drinking so early. She guides me to the table in the corner, his special table. A table that will allow everyone to watch his entrance and force them to turn if they want to sneak a glance at his menu selection.

"He thought you might like some Pellegrino," says the woman. She curls two fingers toward a beautiful young waiter who has no doubt taken the job in hopes of serving salmon tartines to a casting agent. He glides over, displaying teeth so blazingly white that for a moment I think they're blue.

He thought I might like some Pellegrino. Fine.

I nod and the waiter pours a hiss of effervescence from the green glass bottle.

I quickly glance through the menu and give the waiter my selection in advance. I set it aside and retrieve the planner from my purse. I review the notes from the discussion with my client. My client does not want an outside producer. He wants to engineer, produce, and mix the album on his own. I will confirm this today. I will also confirm the budget. I like budgets.

The woman in black reappears. "His car has arrived. He is here," she whispers.

He.

Who is *he*?

He is Mythic Man. A star-maker in the music business and the new record executive for my client.

And he has invited me to lunch.

I am in my midtwenties, out of my depth, and, some would say, out of my mind.

Despite the cost of the valet, I'm looking forward to a productive meeting. It's January and a bit chilly, but I'm warmed by the ivory cashmere turtleneck I scored on the irregulars rack during May Company's liquidation blowout. Mending the hole in the armpit took no time at all.

He enters, celestial, his long hair flowing across his shoulders and linen tunic. He walks just one halting foot at a time because people reach out to stop him, fete him, or shake his hand. They turn to watch, necks extending, to see who sits at his table. I see the ticker of assumed narratives percolating through their minds—I'm the accountant, the personal shopper, or the travel agent.

"You were here early," he says, giving me a kiss on the cheek. "You know I like that."

Staff appears from nowhere to put the napkin on his lap, open a new bottle of Pellegrino, and tell him the chef is so delighted he's back.

"They know me here," he tells me.

"They know you everywhere," I reply.

"Yes, isn't that nice?" He smiles. "Did you see him? Boy Band is here today," he says. "What do you think?"

"That the restaurant shouldn't be serving minors," I tell him. "Liability."

His eyes pull to my planner on the table. "Look at you, all business all the time. They probably think you're my accountant."

"Speaking of numbers . . ."

"Ah, nice budget segue. Effortless. Let me look at the menu first." He lifts the menu and reveals pristinely manicured nails, odd on such large, hairy hands.

The boy with fluorescent teeth stands at the ready. I think he's clenching.

"She'll have . . ."

The waiter sucks in a breath. Mythic Man looks to him.

"She's already ordered."

"Oh, is that so?" Mythic Man looks at me. His brows crimp with curiosity. "Do you have allergies?"

"Only to those who control my lunch," I joke. I hope the humorous lilt in my voice is believable.

I don't dislike this man. I respect his talent and dedication. A lot. But it's important that he sees me as a business colleague. I am an artist manager. In a turtleneck.

The lunch goes well, the discussion even better. We reach an agreement on all things and do so sensibly. We even agree on the budget. I'm thrilled. He seems to be as well.

"Ruta, I enjoy working with you. You're so professional, focused, and dedicated to your clients."

I stare at him. Mythic Man has just given me the greatest compliment. And his compliment is sincere. It cracks the armor. "Thank you," I breathe.

"May I tell you something?" he asks.

"Of course." I nod, abandoning all guard.

"You have so much going for you. Except . . . I don't like your face. You could do something about that, you know."

The couple at the next table looks at me. Fluorescent Teeth looks at me.

My face.

Sure, I have a Baltic nose and sharp features, but I'm in my mid-twenties, supposedly the prime of anyone's youthful beauty. Something is wrong with my face?

I laugh. Probably because somewhere inside I fear I might cry. I lean over the table and give my best look of shock. "I believe you just tried to insult me."

"But you're not insulted. That type of beauty stuff doesn't bother you."

"Nah, I don't have time for it. And let's be honest. It's a budget thing," I say.

And then we both laugh.

Only his laugh—it's genuine.

✳ ✳ ✳

I don't like your face.

No matter how business-minded I was, no matter how hard I tried to fit my square self into the round hole of the music business, I was still human. It was still possible to dent me.

And that rude comment, it dented me. It dented me in the way that exhumes memories and picks at old wounds, that brings back choruses of witchy wart face and ducklings who would look great in a turban. But it didn't hurt for long. I told a friend and after ten minutes we genuinely roared about it, along with the fact that I had driven off and stuck Mythic Man with the bill for my parking. It became a good story. It became a benchmark that no feedback could beat.

Sometimes, people provide input you didn't ask for or expect. Sometimes they give negative, hurtful opinions unrelated to your work, but related to you personally. Remember, they're just one person. And often they're someone who doesn't know you, your life, or your story. There will be so many others who feel differently. There will be Hungarian diesel breathers who bring you flowers, tattooed paratroopers who whisk you away on adventures, and real friends who truly want to lift you up instead of tear you down.

And something important to keep in mind—the way we process feedback is often just a matter of timing, setting, or the perspective we view it from.

Several years after I had left Los Angeles, I returned for an event. And who did I see? Mythic Man. I quickly moved to the opposite corner of the room, hoping to avoid him entirely. But after a few moments he appeared at my side.

"Ruta!" he exclaimed. "So good to see you here."

"Thank you."

"I hear that you're writing now," he said. "And clearly, you're enjoying it. Look at you. You look beautiful. You're smiling. No more serious, frustrated face!"

❋ ❋ ❋

I don't like your face.

That's what he had said.

The way I interpreted *I don't like your face* was *I think you're ugly.*

But with a buffer of time, I realized that's not exactly what he meant.

"I don't like your face. You could do something about that, you know."

If the dialogue had continued maybe he would have said, "I don't like your face. You could do something about that, you know. You could laugh more, Ruta. Relax a bit, Ruta."

I had been working a job that demanded things that didn't align with my true nature. I was in a setting and an industry that required constant shielding and hypervigilance. And unbeknownst to me, that showed on my face. A serious, frustrated face. And Mythic Man recognized my unhappiness before I did.

The calendar pages flip forward. Years pass.

Mythic Man, the restaurant, and many of the record labels are long gone now.

But the memories remain. As do my revised perceptions of them.

Guess what else remains? The cashmere turtleneck. And the mended armpit? The stitch is still holding.

REVISION & INPUT · RECAP

※

- Writing is rewriting. Your work will need revision.

- Revision is a gift, an opportunity to improve your work.

- Writer's block is fear. Give yourself the courage to fail. Write crap. It's just a draft.

- Don't concern yourself with perfection at the outset. Get something down. You'll revise.

- Reassure yourself that it's not final. It's just a draft.

- Put your work aside for a period of time. Come back to it with fresh eyes.

- Ask someone who knows you well, someone you trust, to read your pages and give you feedback.

- Consider finding a reader who represents your target audience.

- Get feedback from readers who are from the same backgrounds, ethnicities, or identities as your characters.

- Check with your local library, bookstore, or professional organizations to see if there are any writing or critique groups in the area that you might join.

- Don't aim to make your manuscript perfect; aim to make it memorable.

- A single review doesn't speak for you, but a catalog of work does.

- Remember, sometimes the way we process feedback has to do with timing, setting, or the angle we view it from.

REVISION & INPUT · WRITING PROMPTS

❧

- Think back to a performance, a competition, or an assignment you wish you could change. Write a scene or description, revising your performance and the outcome.

- The lunch scene with Mythic Man—what if he never showed up? What if he brought someone? List five different ways you could change the plot and revise the lunch scene.

- Revise and expand upon this sentence to show a bit more character development:

  A sentry of a hostess dressed in black quickly steps forward to block my path.

- Revise and expand upon this sentence to show a bit more about the setting:

  The valet takes my car and disappears down San Vicente Boulevard.

Revise the dialogue passage below to imply that I'm timid or fearful instead of annoyed:

"She's already ordered."

"Oh, is that so?" Mythic Man looks at me. His brows crimp with curiosity. "Do you have allergies?"

"Only to those who control my lunch," I joke. I hope the humorous lilt in my voice is believable.

Writer's Block

The condition commonly known as writer's block indicates the inability to produce new creative work. Writer's block affects not only novelists and writers but those in other creative disciplines as well. The causes are many: pressure, illness, stress, expectation, and boredom have all been known to contribute to writer's block.

Q: Who coined the term *writer's block*, and when?

Pepperidge Farm

Founded by Margaret Rudkin amid the Great Depression, Pepperidge Farm is associated with bread and baked goods, but some might be surprised to learn that Pepperidge Farm is a real place. Originally located in Fairfield, Connecticut, and named for the sour gum (pepperidge) tree, the brand grew out of Rudkin's experiments to create minimally processed food that wouldn't aggravate her youngest son's allergies.

Q: When asked what made her company so successful, what was Rudkin's answer?

The Grammy Awards

The Grammy Award is the music industry's highest honor. Presented annually by the Recording Academy, the golden gramophone is selected and awarded by music business peers to recognize the most outstanding achievement in the American music industry. The first Grammy Awards ceremony was held in 1959, and it was first televised live in 1971, but it wasn't until the mid-1980s that Grammy recipients saw a correlation between the award and an increase in sales.

Q: Returning to our Partridge Family reference, they were nominated for a Grammy in 1971. What happened? Did they win?

Cashmere

Cashmere is a form of wool fiber obtained from goats and has been manufactured in Mongolia, Nepal, Kashmir, and Afghanistan for thousands of years. Cashmere is known for both its softness and durable warmth. But not all cashmere is made equal and high prices don't always indicate higher quality.

Q: Why has the production of cashmere wool been criticized?

❧COURAGE❧

Getting Started

WHEN IT COMES TO WRITING, WHAT do you fear?

Perhaps you feel out of your depth, worried you won't follow through, worried you don't have the education, worried about pursuing your own creativity, worried that others will be shocked by what you write, worried that no one will understand.

Or maybe it's this simple—you have no idea where to start.

The word *writing* can be daunting. But the word *story* is not. Why is that?

The two are intertwined, yet the perception is that writing seems to require muse and courage while story is something relegated to the sidecar. But remember, story is always the driver. No matter how confident the writer, if the story is underdeveloped, it won't be memorable.

To kick-start your writing process, play around with a few different structures. I've included several format examples in this book. But what medium will best capture *your* story and memories? Which format might you have the courage to try? Will you incorporate poetry, prose, photographs, illustrations, a list, a letter, emails, or perhaps a hybrid of them all?

Keep in mind that length doesn't make a story memorable. Sometimes, if a story is too lengthy, a reader might take a break and never return to it. You want to create something the reader can't pull away from.

If the idea of writing a full narrative story is too overwhelming, start with a simple list. Choose a subject or memory. Try capturing the story in ten bullet points:

- *Granny Earline. Gone. "A heart attack,"*
  muttered the cop who called.
- *Grabbed a beer and smokes at the Kwik Way.*
  A fake ID still buys real alcohol.
- *Bereavement fare on a filthy Greyhound up to Detroit.*
  Didn't sleep. A heart attack.
- *Washed my black jeans at the laundromat.*
  Cleaned my boots.
- *Walked the highway to the funeral home.*
  Marlboro Reds. Cold rain. Warm jeans.
- *"Sorry. So sorry," whispered the undertaker.*
  "A good woman. Good bean salad."
- *Little Granny in the casket. Granny?*
  The makeup, so thick and pasty around her neck.
- *Her neck. The marks. No . . . not a heart attack.*
- *My name and number—next to Granny's bed,*
  on her fridge, in her purse, in her Bible.
- *"Go back to that mud flap shithole you came from."*
  That's what the cop told me.

Although brief and stuttered, the fictional list above contains plot, obstacles, voice, character detail, and setting. Who killed Granny? A teenager from the rural South who loved her wants to know. But the city cops are hiding something.

If ten bullet points are still too daunting, strive for even tighter economy and use the fabled six-word story method that is often associated with Hemingway. As legend goes, Hemingway bet his drinking buddies that he could write a novel in six words. They took the bet and he took their money when he scribbled the following on a cocktail napkin:

For sale. Baby shoes. Never worn.

Although it's been proven that the six-word story existed well before Hemingway, the legend is perhaps most associated with him because his writing style was often uncluttered and direct. The six-word story is an example of a simple structure and a fun exercise to capture depth and dimension with the fewest words, or *le mot juste*, the exact word, as Flaubert called it.

Below are two examples, whittling our ten bullet points down to just six words.

1. *Granny in the casket. Cops lied.*
2. *Cops lied, Granny. I tried, Granny.*

How would you create a better and more compact version of the ten bullet points?

Every story commands its own particular structure. But in the beginning, don't concern yourself with final framework. Instead, use techniques to mine memories that ignite sparks of emotion and inspiration. Once you find something you're interested in writing about, begin scribbling lists or experimenting with dialogue just for fun. Or write just one sentence per day. A single sentence can contain deep truths. A single sentence might be a story unto itself.

It might also help to read a few pieces in a tighter format, such as short stories or flash fiction. Flash fiction, also known as microfiction, can involve just a few words up to a few hundred, and generally takes only two or three minutes to read. Would a simplified structure feel more manageable for your project?

Perhaps structure isn't the fear. Maybe you're worried about being "seen" if you write through a memory. If you want to write about a personal experience but feel hesitant to do so, consider researching autofiction. Autofiction combines autobiography and fiction. Through autofiction you might be able to write about something memorable but make it unrecognizable to others who are familiar with the person or event. In other words, autofiction might allow you write about Uncle Ron's nudist colony experiment without hurting his feelings or getting yourself blackballed from the family.

But being seen and *feeling* seen are very different. Being seen implies being observed, while feeling seen carries resolution and peace, doesn't it? Think of a rare moment when you may have felt seen and understood by the world or those around you. What did that feel like?

Maybe it was fleeting. Maybe it was long in coming. Or maybe it was through an interaction with a stranger. Sometimes those who claim to know us don't really know us at all, right? And yet a chance encounter with an outsider momentarily puts the earth back on its axis in a way you hope to remember forever. That's still how I explain the random incident at seventeen when

I kissed the gas station attendant—kissed him as if the world were ending, for the record.

Have you ever felt seen by a stranger?

Of course, sometimes the process of feeling seen, or being able to write about it, takes a while. Maybe even years.

Two days prior to my high school commencement, the school held a celebration assembly in the gymnasium. The seniors sat on metal folding chairs, flanked by younger students, parents, and families in the bleachers, mine included. There were announcements, jokes, speeches, and our class rock star performed the tune we had chosen as our class song.

Amid the revelry were the announcements of class superlatives: Most Likely to Succeed, Best Dressed, Wittiest, Biggest Flirt, Most Athletic, etc. Some were complimentary, some were funny, some were not. But the senior class had voted on them during lunch period the week prior. Was it important? This was how our fellow classmates saw one another and might remember one another, right?

My name wouldn't be called. After all, no one truly understood me. Right?

But my name *was* called. And it wasn't for the category of Class Historian or Most Studious. No, no. Mine had more in common with the pole dancer boots I mentioned earlier. The seniors hooted and howled. The younger students stomped their feet in the bleachers.

Me?

I was stunned. I was thrilled.

Thrilled!

I often felt misunderstood. And that feeling flung me into

brown chapters and pity parties. But of all the superlatives they could have selected, my classmates chose something I thought not many knew about me.

I was so excited, I ran to the podium, nearly tripping over my white Payless pumps to grab that hand-drawn certificate. I held it to my chest, smiling amid the claps and whistles.

It concerned my father but delighted my mother. Later, there was family dialogue about it.

"That award. The reaction. I'm not sure that's a compliment," said my father gently. "Of course it is," insisted Mom. "The men in the Cayman Islands said the same thing to Ruta. They clapped and hooted for her, remember? And she was only eleven then."

To me it was a compliment. The superlative—it's probably not how my classmates would remember me now, but that's okay. Because at that moment, after four difficult years of high school, I suddenly felt seen and understood. My soul exhaled. And that fleeting moment in the gym, it filled me with peace and gave me courage to move on. To move forward. To search for stories and share them in a way that might make others feel seen, too.

Very few of us have a howling pen that writes pure brilliance. No. Most of us scale walls of fear and stumble in the wrong shoes while trying to find our way. We worry about what our family might think. We make plans but lose our nerve. We sit on the edge, dangling our feet but not daring to jump. But one day, we come to realize that creativity and imagination are forms of courage. When embraced, creativity and imagination kick fear out of the ring.

Yes, there will be challenge. There will be revelation and transformation. That's the hero's journey.

That is courage. That is memory. That is story.

So take a breath and do it.

Jump.

The Emotion of Memory

PERHAPS YOU FEEL THAT YOU DON'T have memorable, plot-worthy experiences to draw from. But in truth, memories are built from emotions, and everyone has experienced emotions. Reflecting on those sentiments can inspire recollection and unearth long-lost details. Of course, as with any writing or creative exercise, be gentle with yourself and use your own best judgment in deciding which emotions to return to. Excavating memories can be painful. Some are best left alone or postponed for a time when you can view them through a lens of strength. But if you feel up for it, reflect on a few emotions.

Think of a time you felt jealous. There's a story there that includes plot, setting, character, and perspective. How would you describe it?

Can you recall a time when you felt nervous? What was the situation, where did it take place, and who was involved? Did your body respond physically? If so, how?

Have you ever felt skeptical or suspicious? Who were the characters involved and where did your suspicion take you? Did your inklings prove correct?

Confusion. Fear. Surprise. They're all sensations that hold stories. Jot a few paragraphs about them. Consider compound emotions as well. Compounding presents the power of juxtaposition mentioned earlier. Something can be beautiful yet sad. You can feel reluctant yet hopeful. Have you ever experienced something that's funny but also uncomfortable? I have.

My parents had decided to leave Michigan and move south to be closer to family. It was agreed that my father would handle the business transfer and Mom would start the initial process of house hunting. I agreed to assist.

"Schedule a midday showing in the country club," said my mother.

"Mom, you're not buying in the country club."

"No, but they'll invite us for a free lunch if we listen to their spiel. Country clubs have great chicken salad."

So off to the country club we went. I was hesitant, but also curious. We drove down the long, manicured drive to the entry gate and suddenly, I felt nervous.

"I'm not sure about this, Mom."

"Trust me, these young people, they have a quota. They need to report that they've met with a certain number of prospective buyers. We'll be helping them."

The club staff was entirely delighted with Mom. Charmed by her spunk and pageboy haircut. A member of the marketing team showed us their available inventory and sure enough, they asked us to stay for lunch. The chicken salad was very good, but as soon as we finished, I wanted to leave. Mom wasn't quite ready.

"Tell me about yourself, Hailey," said Mom to the young sales agent. "Do you love it here? Are you achieving all that you've hoped? Is there a dessert menu? I'd love a cup of coffee."

The young woman was eager to share, but mooching the

meal? It didn't feel right. I felt uncomfortable. But I also felt judgmental. How could I disparage Mom? Was I being a hypocrite? When I first moved to Los Angeles, there were no restaurant meals with Mythic Man. I was on a minuscule budget and at that age, entertainment outranked food on my priority list. So instead of buying groceries, I grazed the supermarket samples. Gelson's. Erewhon. Trader Joe's. They all gave out tastings of the luxury food products they were trying to sell. I was too poor to be a picky eater.

"Would you like to try the liver pâté?"

"Oh, yes please," I'd say without hesitation. "Is there a cracker?"

My serial sample tastings—was that so different from what Mom was doing?

My mother filled out a comment card before leaving. She raved about Hailey's professionalism and the delicious decaf. "Feedback is very important," she told me.

Mom didn't drive but was always game to explore. Juxtaposition, anyone? Her spirit of adventure was also how we ended up at the home of an NFL player—an early draft pick who had fallen on hard times and needed to dump his thirty-acre estate.

"Oh, Ruta. We must see this one. It will be outrageous."

Mom loved outrageous. Delighted in it.

And she was right. It was outrageous. Six thousand square feet on the main level alone. Floor-to-ceiling dirty windows, piles of abandoned athletic equipment, and several fountains spitting green scum. The littered mansion was massive. And my mother sashayed through it, sniffer in the air, opening cupboards and evaluating bathrooms as if ready to pull out her checkbook.

"Lovely cabinetry. Soft-close drawers," she commented. She threw me a mischievous glance and proceeded to the bedrooms.

She opened the closets. All of them. And took her time inspecting.

"Mom, don't," I whispered. My stomach tightened. It was too much.

"Don't what? This is an open house. Storage space is important," she said, poking her narrow loafer through a heap of trash bags stuffed in the closet. "What's in all of these black garbage bags?" she whispered. "Aren't you even curious?"

"I'm uncomfortable. Let's go," I pleaded.

Mom elbowed me, motioning to several framed game jerseys astride empty beer bottles. "He could have sold the jerseys on eBay," she tsked. "And more black garbage bags. All full. Very suspicious, don't you think?"

We walked back to the kitchen where the sales agent was speaking with a group of prospective buyers.

"The estate is being sold as is. The owner is very motivated," explained the agent. "If interested, please submit your best offer. We expect this to go quickly. Any questions?"

"Yes," said my mother. "Any deaths on the property that should be disclosed?"

The sales agent looked at us.

The attendees all turned and looked at us.

"Well, there are a *lot* of black garbage bags," said Mom.

Oh my gosh. Any deaths on the property? Did she really just say that? I was so uncomfortable. And a bit annoyed. But the way my mother stood, waiting in all seriousness for a reply to her murder inquiry, I suddenly wanted to burst out laughing. Did she really think the black garbage bags were full of dead bodies?

Hesitant. Curious. Nervous. Judgmental. Uncomfortable. Annoyed. Entertained.

When I recall those compound feelings, the door to memory opens and suddenly details of the experience spill forth. And they're all elements that can enhance scenes within my writing. The Band-Aid on the agent's neck that didn't quite hide the hickey. The busted maracas and the dirty Crock-Pot on the bedroom floor. The thunderstorm on the drive home. Mom's laughter. And suddenly dialogue and conversation return.

"Wait, wait, wait. What if those garbage bags were full of money?" breathed Mom.

"He was a cornerback, not a bookie, Mom."

I can also hear the voice of the suspicious agent. "Could you sign the register and include the name of your agent, please? We'll share the disclosures once you've made an offer."

Mom happily obliged. But instead of our real estate agent, Mom listed Bill Bonesack, our old handyman who had been dead for a decade.

Thinking back on that day, it makes me laugh. And as I now write about being uncomfortable yet amused, annoyed yet amazed by my mom's audacity, other sentiments begin to push in.

Longing. I would give anything to have one more day with my mom. I'm a writer, yet I find it painfully difficult to describe how much I miss her.

Understanding. If only I could tell Mom that I now understand. Her audacity and humor—that was her way of trying to coax me out of my worried world. "Don't be so serious," she begged constantly. "You've gotta have some fun."

Disbelief. How life can turn cruel, and how unfair death can feel. I can't always muster the courage to return to the memories.

Delight. How my incredible and hilarious mother lives on through those who tell stories about her. My friend recently said, "Some claim cardinals are the departed, returning to say hello. If I see a cardinal sitting on a branch smoking a cigarette, I'll know it's your mom."

The image of a cardinal smoking a Kent Ultra Light? Mom would love that. I hope I've included enough murder and cigarettes in this book to please her.

Perhaps you can relate to some of what I describe? On the following page, I've included a list of feelings. It's not comprehensive, of course, but as you scroll through the list, make note of those that jump out at you and bring a story to mind. Are they isolated or connected to another feeling on the list? If so, why?

Experience is less about where we've traveled and worked, or what we've seen. It's more about our feelings. Reflecting on your interior life and your emotions leads back to story and to the realization that no matter what your age, if you've felt deeply, you've lived deeply. And in that way, you are a courageous person of deep experience. And when we acknowledge the infinite number of emotions that we're capable of feeling, we realize that there are an infinite number of ways to feel—and be—human. That's beautiful.

And that's worth writing about.

LIST OF FEELINGS

Abandoned. Afraid. Angry. Annoyed.
Apprehensive. Ashamed. Astonished. Awkward.

Bashful. Bereaved. Bewildered. Bitter.
Blissful. Bold. Bored. Bothered. Brave.

Calm. Capable. Carefree. Cautious.
Compulsive. Confident. Confused. Cranky. Curious.

Daring. Defiant. Delighted. Depressed.
Disappointed. Discouraged. Disgusted.

Ecstatic. Edgy. Embarrassed. Empty.
Energetic. Enraged. Envious. Excited. Extravagant.

Fatigued. Fearful. Flustered. Foolish.
Forgiving. Free. Frustrated. Funny. Furious.

Generous. Gloomy. Grateful. Greedy.
Grief-stricken. Grumpy. Guilty

(Oh, the *H*'s!)
Happy. Heartbroken. Helpless. Hesitant. Horrified.
Humbled. Humiliated. Hungry. Hurt.

Ignorant. Impatient. Inferior. Inquisitive. Insecure.
Inspired. Irrational. Irritated. Isolated.

Jaded. Jealous. Jittery.
Joyful. Judged. Judgmental.

Kind.

Lazy. Lonely. Loving.

Mad. Manipulated. Marvelous. Mean.
Melodramatic. Mischievous. Misunderstood.

Naive. Nasty. Needy. Neglected.
Nervous. Nice. Nonchalant. Numb.

Obedient. Obligated. Obsessive.
Offended. Open-minded. Overjoyed. Overwhelmed.

Panicked. Patient. Peaceful. Pensive.
Petty. Powerless. Pressured. Proud. Puzzled.

Qualified. Quarrelsome.
Questioning. Quiet. Quirky.

Rebellious. Rejuvenated. Relaxed. Relieved.
Reluctant. Repulsed. Resentful. Restless.

Sad. Safe. Selfish. Shocked. Shy. Skeptical.
Stressed. Stubborn. Surprised. Suspicious.

Tearful. Terrified. Thankful. Threatened.
Tolerant. Tolerated. Torn. Touched. Trusting.

Unafraid. Uncomfortable. Undecided.
Understood. Unimpressed. Useful. Useless.

Vacant. Vain. Valuable. Vibrant.
Victorious. Volatile. Vulnerable.

Wary. Weak. Whiny. Wishful.
Witty. Worldly. Worried. Worthless. Wronged.

Xenophobic.

Yearning. Yielding. Youthful.

Zany. Zealous.

COURAGE · RECAP

- To kick-start your writing process, play around with a few different structures.

- Give thought to what sort of medium might best capture your story and memories. Poetry, prose, photographs, a combination?

- In the beginning, use techniques to mine memories that ignite sparks of emotion and inspiration.

- Start with simple assignments. A list, or just one paragraph.

- Choose words that capture dimension. A single sentence can be a story unto itself.

- Sometimes, the process of feeling seen, or being able to write about it, takes a while. Maybe even years. And some emotions might be best avoided altogether. Give yourself time and space.

- Creativity and imagination are forms of courage.

- Think of ways to preserve your story and memories for the future, when you might return to write about them.

- Emotions are the building blocks of story and experience.

- To feel deeply is the essence of being human.

COURAGE · WRITING PROMPTS

- When it comes to writing, what do you fear? Make a list.

- Choose a topic or memory. Write a story in ten bullet points.

- Rewrite the story of Granny Earline in six words, two different ways.

- Think back to a time you felt seen. Write a paragraph about it.

- Review Joseph Campbell's structure of the hero's journey. Is the framework referencing classical myths and legends primarily for male heroes? How might you update and expand upon it to be more inclusive and reflective of contemporary society?

- Create a list of secret superlatives about yourself—things that no one else knows. Most Likely to Lose a Finger While Cooking? Best Shower Singer? Biggest Anchovy Fan?

❧ Using a secret superlative, create a voicemail message from my mom. Remember, the structure goes like this: "Hi, love, it's me. [Insert some terrible, horrible news + thought.] Buh-bye!"

Hi, love, it's me. Remember the time you cut off your index finger? Sushi knives are bad news. Buh-bye!

Hemingway

American writer Ernest Hemingway was known for many things: novels, short stories, journalism, hunting, adventure, and his love of cats. Hemingway had dozens of cats, all with unique names to honor or identify them. Hemingway's feline friends included Snow White, Princess Six-Toes, Furhouse, and his favorite, Boise. Many of Hemingway's cats were polydactyl, because he considered them good luck.

Q: What's a polydactyl cat?

Flaubert

Perhaps best known for his novel *Madame Bovary*, French novelist Gustave Flaubert originally went to Paris to study law but abandoned his studies to pursue writing instead. Flaubert is well known for his painstaking perfectionism. He insisted that his writing was the result of incredibly hard work, revision, and his search for *le mot juste*—the exact word.

Q: Why was *Madame Bovary* banned upon publication in 1856?

Combinatory Play

Creativity is combinatory. While creating, we paste, braid, combine, and recombine elements to generate new ideas. Theoretical physicist Albert Einstein referred to this approach as "combinatory play" and described it as the act of opening one mental channel by dabbling in another. Combinatory play can be particularly helpful in sourcing new ideas and options when feeling stuck. Einstein, for example, reported having many breakthroughs in physics while playing his violin.

Q: True or false? During Einstein's autopsy, his brain was removed for preservation without the permission of his family.

The Hero's Journey

The hero's journey is a story template composed of three stages and seventeen steps to establish, challenge, and deliver the protagonist home. The structure was originally derived from Joseph Campbell's 1949 work, *The Hero with a Thousand Faces*, through which he examines the concepts of myths, legends, and the archetypal hero. Campbell's template was embraced in Hollywood after George Lucas announced he used the framework as a model for *Star Wars*.

Q: What was Joseph Campbell's famous mantra for a meaningful life?

CONCLUSION

YOU'RE STILL UNCONVINCED. No one could ever understand you.

But think of it this way: What if exploring your memories could be a vehicle for understanding not only you, but someone else? What if exploring your memories helps heal something painful by expressing it or transforming it into something better on the page? What if your characters can communicate something in your story that you weren't able to communicate in real life? What if exploring your memories helps you resolve something you think no one will understand? If your song remains unsung, hiding within you, you make sure that no one ever will.

Why does that matter?

When we share our stories, we open ourselves to connection, and it's moments of connection that make life richer. They deepen the human experience. And knowledge of story eliminates speculation. Consider this:

There's an older gentleman, living alone in the neighborhood. The narrative and formed opinion of the man is that he's unsocial, kind of grumpy. He rarely attends neighborhood functions and has never been to the annual fireworks display that is so carefully planned by the community. A story sprouts that the man is unpatriotic. After all, who doesn't like the Fourth of July? The narrative takes root. It's accepted and adopted by others.

One day the man is getting his mail and a little boy skids up on his bicycle.

"Hi, Mr. Jonas. I'm Jesse. Is it true that you're unpatriotic? They say you're a communist, whatever that is."

The old man's eyes expand with shock. "Goodness no, I'm not unpatriotic, and I'm certainly not a communist."

"Then why don't you come to the fireworks?"

The man tents his hands and brings them to his lips. He takes a breath before responding.

"Well, when I was your age, Jesse, there was a war going on. My family was on a list of those to be killed. We actually had to escape from the communists. I had to leave my country, my friends, and my extended family. I spent many years in a refugee camp, and during the war, the areas surrounding the camp were repeatedly bombed. I saw everything explode. It was terrifying."

Now it is the boy's eyes that are expanding.

"Yes. So you see, on the Fourth of July, the sound of fireworks reminds me of the bombings. Over seventy years have passed, but for some reason, that sound—it activates the old feeling of fear in me." The man's eyes wrinkle with emotion. "I don't want to make others uncomfortable or burden them with my story. So I just avoid the fireworks. Does that make sense?"

Jesse nods slowly. He then takes off on his bicycle and the old man hears him yelling to the kids down the street. "Hey, guys, guess what! Mr. Jonas was bombed!"

The kids tell the other kids. They tell their parents. The parents tell other adults. And suddenly, the atmosphere in the neighborhood around the old man shifts from criticism to compassion. And admiration.

All because they know his story.

He isn't unpatriotic. He isn't a communist. He is a survivor who still struggles with painful memories. The old man didn't want to burden the neighbors with his story. But in remaining quiet, he created a burden of misjudgment and perhaps a burden of loneliness.

If we don't know a person's story, sometimes we create one of our own. And in doing so, we might misjudge them. Knowledge of story helps classrooms, communities, companies, and countries function not only better, but more compassionately. What is the story of your community or the schools you've attended? Do you know the history of the country your neighbor is from? Do you know their story? Do they know yours? Thinking back, I never introduced myself to my neighbors in Los Angeles. I never gave them a chance to get to know me. Could my experience in LA have been different if I had?

Throughout this book I've presented some elementary building blocks of story. And in doing so, I've layered in elements and vignettes of my own story to illustrate. I've used varied structures to share the *H*'s of heartbreak, hope, hilarity, and humiliation. You've been introduced to various people, plots, and events that have played a role in my life. I've left some lingering questions, to keep you, the reader, thinking and inspired to investigate.

How long would it take, for example, to uncover that when I was awarded the superlative of Best Dancer in high school, what was very audibly announced was Best Exotic Dancer—which in those days was the equivalent of crowning me Best Stripper!

Fantastic, right? Peeling and stripping back layers of memory, that is.

There are infinite ways to write books and share stories. There's not just one way; there's your way. But creativity is combinatory. When we create something, we combine our inspirations, memories, knowledge, talents, dreams, and emotions. We mold and shape thoughts, revise ideas, and discover new ways to view old feedback. And then we sew it all together into a new project. Who knows, maybe the real-life setting was New York, not Los Angeles, Cliff was actually Cathy, and the Mythic Man was really a Wonder Woman. You can share the elements in a multitude of ways, but what matters most to your readers is how the story makes them feel.

So choose each word carefully, understand what your character wants, bring the story to life with detail. And don't rely on muse. Sure, muse is amazing when in residence, but where is she when you're trapped at two hundred pages beneath the weight of a soggy middle? When the muse runs off to Reno, you'll need motivation and work ethic to make it across the finish line. You'll need to be limber enough to kick yourself in the pants. Muse is too unreliable.

Instead, cling tight to that essential, core element mentioned at the very beginning:

Heart.

Heart is a connector. And that's the goal: to facilitate deeper understanding through story and memory. That brings us closer. If we never share our story, we cement ourselves into a place of certainty that no one will ever understand. It's difficult to escape from cement. Ask Jimmy Hoffa.

Poet Maxine Kumin said, "We are, each of us, our own prisoner. We are locked up in our own story."

That statement conveys the intensity of personal history and remembering. But instead of being trapped in our own experience and memories, could we use them to make the world less lonely for ourselves and others? I'll leave you with this final example.

When I published my first novel, *Between Shades of Gray*, I was certain very few would understand. A story about a Lithuanian teenager deported to a death camp in Siberia? That's not exactly commercial fare. I didn't have exact details of my own family's experience in Siberia, but I hoped to share the general history. I truly didn't know if anyone would understand. Or care.

But they did.

Readers were moved by the harrowing plight of those described in the book. They were shocked that the story and history was so widely unknown. But nearly every Lithuanian or Baltic family had been touched by deportation. And when the book was published, they stepped forward to share their stories. While on book tour I met Lithuanians in Ohio, Michigan, Illinois, Nebraska, Florida, California, Massachusetts, and many countries around the world. I met dozens of women and children named Ruta, and countless families who shared histories similar to my own.

Elderly readers came to events and with quivering voices told me that they remembered my grandfather and his teachings. How my grandmother had shared her knitting needles. A stranger brought me a picture of my father as a little boy in the refugee camp. And imagine the tears when I received a phone call from a man who said, "I think I have something for you."

This man of no relation, he had the details and missing pieces. He had discovered old letters in a basement that revealed my family's experience in Siberia.

I still get emotional thinking about it. When we go searching for history and memory, the universe responds and our history begins searching for us. My desire to share a story—it led me back to my own story. And suddenly, the world went from feeling vast and separate to very close and intimately meaningful. People gathered at events. We laughed together and cried together.

We shared our stories.

As you come to the end of this book, I hope you've been introduced to some very basic concepts of plot, character development, setting, dialogue, voice, and how memory can fuel creativity and connection. You now know that I lock my door when it rains. And if you ever hear someone say, "Hi, Ruta. How was your flight?" we can share a knowing look and a laugh. Because you'll probably have a much deeper understanding of what that question means to me than the person who's asking. You know the backstory, the conflict layers.

Yes, writing takes courage. And time. But memories are like leaves. They fade, fall, and scatter beneath the slightest sigh of wind. So for now, think of ways to press them between wax paper and preserve them for one quiet day in the future. And on that day, as you retrieve your memories, may you rediscover and celebrate the glorious combination of details that not only make you beautiful, but also make you uniquely *YOU*.

Your story.

GRATITUDE

MANY AUTHORS WRITE AND SUCCEED ON their own. I am not one of those authors.

Kacie Wheeler and Jeffrey Kirkland manage my days and events with loving care. While sitting in my office and laughing about my random life adventures, Kacie suddenly decided that I must write a book about writing and share some of my *own* stories. Kacie and Jeff each read multiple drafts. They've laughed and cried with me through significant life events. They know these stories—and know there are many more.

Steven Malk is not only an incredible agent, he's an incredible human. My spectacular and tireless editor, Tamar Brazis, guided and helped shape this book, and Meriam Metoui provided invaluable insight. Ken Wright, Jen Loja, Shanta Newlin, Felicia Frazier, Emily Romero, Carmela Iaria, Kim Ryan, Liza Kaplan, and everyone at Penguin has championed my work for over a decade. Theresa Evangelista created the gorgeous cover, and Lucia Baez designed the interior. Kelley Salas and Krista Ahlberg handled the copyediting.

My critique group of nearly twenty years—Sharon Cameron, Amy Eytchison, Howard Shirley, and Angelika Stegmann. I could never do it without them and would never want to.

Beth Kephart has been a dear friend and writing mentor for many years. When the pandemic necessitated that I remain home, I immediately signed up for Beth's virtual writing series. That series set me on course for this book.

I owe much love and gratitude to my music clients who allowed me to be their manager. Thank you for the journey, the inspiration, and the education: Desmond Child, Steve Vai, Hair of the Dog, Lit, Niels Bye Nielsen, Eric Sardinas, Kes, Danny Peck, Eric Church, JT Harding, Plumb, and Rhansum.

To those who worked with me and experienced the misadventures of a lifetime: Michael Anthony, Mike Cortese, Ken Phillips, Yvonne Seivertson, the Robleys, Gerry Rosenblatt, Pam Dancy, Curtis Shaw, Winston Simone, Tommy Vinton, Jonathan Watkins, Dan Schmidt, Marius Markevicius, Court Stevens, Christopher Dalston, Brian Greenbaum, Matt Messer, Michael Mesker, Shawn Card, Priscila Bara, Melissa Ortiz, and Donny Broadway.

The list of those who tolerated me as a mime and have cheered me on through the years is endless. Eternally grateful to all of my friends, neighbors, teachers, students, extended family, Michigan, Tennessee, and California pals. Rockets forever.

Sincere thanks to everyone at Penguin Random House, Writers House, Marks Law Group, UTA, Nina Douglas Ltd., Luum, and SCBWI. And of course, the readers, educators, and booksellers.

John and Kristina are my heroes and the best siblings a little sis could ask for. How blessed we were to have such incredible and unique parents. Believe it. Buh-bye!

And Michael, whose love gives me the courage and the wings. He is the heart of my story.

REFERENCES

Ackroyd, Peter. *Blake: A Biography*. New York: Alfred A. Knopf, 1996.

Austen, Jane. *Persuasion*. London: Penguin Classics, 2003.

Borges, Jorge Luis. *In Praise of Darkness*. New York: Dutton, 1974.

Bunnell, Lee. "Tin Man." All rights administered by Warner Chappell Music Inc. (ASCAP).

Campbell, Joseph. *The Hero with a Thousand Faces*. New York: MJF Books, 1949.

Chapman, Tracy L. "Fast Car." All rights administered by Purple Rabbit Music (ASCAP).

Crews, Harry. *A Childhood: The Biography of a Place*. New York: Harper & Row Publishers, 1978.

Daly, Blair; Gillmor, Ryan Joseph; Popoff, Alan Jay; Popoff, Jeremy Alan. "The Broken." All rights administered by 506 Music (ASCAP), EMI April Music (ASCAP), Liberal Arts Music (ASCAP), Litsalright Music (ASCAP), Internal Combustion Music (BMI), Jeremy Popoff Songs (BMI), Kickin' Grids Music (BMI), Seeker from the Speaker Music (BMI), Southside Independent Music Publishing (BMI).

Dickinson, Emily. Personal letter to Frances and Louise Norcross. June 1872.

Eliot, T. S. "Little Gidding." London: Faber and Faber, 1942.

Estés, Clarissa Pinkola, PhD. *Women Who Run With the Wolves: Myths and Stories of the Wild Woman Archetype*. New York: Ballantine Books, 1992.

Fante, John. *Ask the Dust*. New York: Stackpole Sons, 1939.

Ferrucci, Piero. *The Power of Kindness: The Unexpected Benefits of Leading a Compassionate Life*. New York: Penguin Publishing Group, 2006.

Flaubert, Gustave. *La Correspondance de Flaubert; Etude et Repertoire Critique*. Edited by Charles Carlut. Columbus: Ohio State University Press, 1968.

Forster, E. M. *Aspects of the Novel*. London: Edwin Arnold, 1927.

Gaiman, Neil. *Coraline*. New York: Harper Collins, 2002.

Hill, Richard. "Kerouac at the End of the Road." *New York Times*, May 29, 1988.

Jung, C. G. *Archetypes and the Collective Unconscious. The Collected Works of C. G. Jung Volume 9*. 2nd edition. New Jersey: Princeton University Press, 1969.

Kephart, Beth. *We Are the Words: The Master Memoir Class*. Philadelphia: Juncture Workshops, 2021.

Kumin, Maxine W. *The Retrieval System: Poems*. New York: Viking Press, 1978.

Lamott, Anne. "12 Truths I Learned from Life and Writing." Vancouver, British Columbia: TED Talk, 2017.

Morrison, Toni. *Beloved*. New York: Alfred A. Knopf, 1987.

Myss, Caroline. *Sacred Contracts: Awakening Your Divine Potential*. New York: Three Rivers Press, 2002.

Nabokov, Vladimir. *Lolita*. New York: G. P. Putnam's Sons, 1955.

Patchett, Ann. *This Is the Story of a Happy Marriage*. New York: Harper, 2013.

Sedaris, David. "The Old Lady Down the Hall." *Esquire*, October 2000.

Serling, Rod. *The Twilight Zone*. Seasons 4 & 5. 1963–1964.

Walker, Alice. *The Color Purple*. New York: Harcourt Brace Jovanovich, 1982.

Wharton, Edith. *Ethan Frome*. New York: Charles Scribner's Sons, 1911.

White, E. B. *Charlotte's Web*. New York: Harper & Row, 1952.